Alone With Others

Alone With Others

AN EXISTENTIAL APPROACH TO BUDDHISM

STEPHEN BATCHELOR

FOREWORD BY JOHN BLOFELD

Grove Press
New York

Published simultaneously in Canada
Printed in the United States of America

Library of Congress Cataloging-in-Publication Data

Batchelor, Stephen.
Alone with others.

(Grove Press Eastern philosophy and literature series)
Bibliography:
I. Buddhism—Doctrines.   I. Title.   II. Series.
BQ4150.B37   1983   294.3'42   82-21054

ISBN 978-0-8021-5127-8
eIBSN 978-0-8021-9648-4

Grove Press
an imprint of Grove/Atlantic, Inc.
154 West 14th Street
New York, NY 10011

Distributed by Publishers Group West

www.groveatlantic.com

15 16 17 18   15 14 13 12

To my mother

ACKNOWLEDGMENTS

I would like to thank the following people who have contributed in various ways to the completion of this work:
H. H. The XIV Dalai Lama; Geshé Rabten; Geshé Ngawang Dargyey; the students of Tharpa Choeling, Center for Tibetan Studies, Switzerland; Anila Anne Ansermett; Frau Dora Kalff; Dr. Martin Kalff; Herr Richard Gassner; the Tibetisches Zentrum, Hamburg; Professor Herbert V. Guenther; Dr. Michael Levin; John Blofeld; and Hannelore Rosset.

CONTENTS

FOREWORD

When first requested to write this Foreword, I felt truly honored on account of my deep respect for the author's scholarship. Nevertheless, my initial instinct was to decline the honor rather than spend much time on a book which, as I then supposed, must by its very nature cause my reactions to be largely negative. Still, I was compelled by a sense of courtesy to give it at least a cursory glance. To my surprise, that cursory glance led to my reading every paragraph with careful attention and to my being unable to put it down until I had devoured the whole rich banquet at a sitting. Meanwhile, my dinner lay congealing in the dishes, so impossible was it to interrupt a task at once so pleasant, so exciting and, in a way, so portentous!

My initial reluctance stemmed from a personal reaction to a good many books in the category of contemporary formulation of traditional Buddhist doctrines. Of course there are many, and by no means all of them have come my way; but most of those I have read (or at least skipped through) have shocked me—almost to the point of un-Buddhist anger! Many of them reduce the Buddha Dharma to what Stephen Batchelor very rightly terms 'nebulous eclecticism.' A smaller number, including the works of certain erudite Buddhist scholars, employ the grotesque jargon—barely comprehensible to most people—recently evolved to express fresh concepts relating to the 'new sciences' that purport to further our knowledge of the workings of the human mind. Worse still, those otherwise admirable scholars use these gobbledygook terms to convey the meaning of ancient Sanskrit, Tibetan, and Chinese phrases and concepts. (Is it not impermissible to equate traditional concepts poetically expressed with newly coined terms which, besides being uncouth rather than mellifluous like the originals, have been coined specifically to convey concepts not accessible to ancient writers?) Another consideration that has hitherto made me wary of attempts to present Buddhism in contemporary guise is that reformists, however good their intentions, so often 'let out the baby with the bathwater' and thus throw away what is valuable along with the trashy accretions surrounding it.

Well, despite my misgivings, I called to mind that Stephen Batchelor is a remarkable and rather rare kind of person. He has studied Buddhism the hard way, struggling with difficult Tibetan texts, and listening hour after hour, day after day, to oral expositions by learned Tibetans which, though intrinsically precious and illuminating, are often delivered in a manner that requires patience and determination on the part of their pupils. Furthermore, he has the gift of being able to render difficult Eastern concepts into pellucid English, and has a training that enables him to observe the strict requirements of good scholarship. In particular, his translations of Shantideva's *Bodhisattvacaryavatara* (*A Guide to the Bodhisattva's Way of Life*) had left an indelible mark on my mind as one of the most important works in the entire range of English translations of Buddhist texts.

All this should have been enough to dispel my doubts, but I was at the time dubious about the purpose of this new work from an admittedly illustrious pen, namely to describe the development of certain central Buddhist concepts with the help of terminology and methodology devised by exponents of existentialist religion (mainly Christian) and philosophy. The works of Heidegger, Tillich, MacQuarrie, and their confrères do not abound in Bangkok's concrete jungles. Being ignorant of them, I feared more gobbledygook. I was apprehensive, too, that such a book would prove to be yet another example of the pitfalls besetting those who, desiring to promote mutual understanding among the followers of diverse religions, inadvertently distort the separate traditions by pressing them into mutual conformity and thus give an impression of there being more common ground among them than in fact exists. Happily, these fears were soon swept away by study of the typescript: no gobbledygook, no distortion of Buddhist doctrines, but a restatement of them in terms likely to appeal to readers hitherto disinclined to study Buddhism because of its 'foreign' appearance and its *seeming* remoteness from their own lives.

Having spent almost all my adult life in Asia, I have tried in my own books to convey the very 'feel' of Taoism and of Chinese and Tibetan Buddhism when encountered in their native habitat. I like to think this approach has a certain charm for readers attracted by the mellow beauty of Chinese culture and/or the more dramatic colorfulness of Tibetan culture, as well as by the wisdom enshrined in both. However, such an approach has three important limitations. First, it may be ignored by readers quite uninterested in Eastern cultures *per se*, but who would nevertheless be attracted to Buddhism if they were led to discover in it universal verities of pressing concern to them personally. Second, it does too little in the way of assisting people engaged in the transplantation of Buddhism to various parts of the world where it cannot, if its outer aspects remain highy exotic, survive for long in societies more interested in revitalizing their own way of life than in adopting foreign ways. Third, though I tend strongly in the direction of traditionalism, I do realize how impossible it is to accept *everything* my wise Chinese and Tibetan teachers have told me; for a part of their exposition of the Buddha Dharma is likely to derive from local cultural accretions. I recognize that most Western Buddhists in Asia face this particular difficulty.

An amusing but very extreme example of this third point is as follows. I was once warned by a learned Tibetan *geshé* (doctor of religion) that if the thumbs are not tucked out of sight between the joined palms when the hands are placed together in the traditional Buddhist gesture of reverence, so as to make of the hands a 'lotus bud', the offender will be reborn as a black spider! Now that *geshé* was learned enough and sufficiently skilled in debate to have shone during a discussion with, say, Oxford professors on any of several abstruse subjects; yet his extraordinary concretizations of the implications of certain doctrines entirely acceptable in themselves would have rightly drawn smiles of ridicule from ten-year-old English schoolboys! Naturally, most of the hindrances to *total* acceptance of what one's Eastern teachers may impart are of a much more subtle nature than this ludicrous example. I have no wish to belittle my teachers' general wisdom and common sense.

Stephen Batchelor, in the present work, offers a method of propounding the Buddha Dharma in a way that helps to cope with all the difficulties just outlined, and may provide a new impetus to the propagation of Buddhism. His approach is likely to appeal to many categories of readers who have hitherto never considered Buddhism as having great relevance to themselves. He points out that all thinking people sooner or later become aware of disturbing facts and questions which just have to be faced, no matter how reluctantly. They include:

I was alone at birth; I must die alone; and, in a sense, I am always alone, for the gulf separating me from others can never satisfactorily be bridged.

Alas, death is life's only certainty. Besides making me apprehensive because I cannot know what follows, it causes me present anxiety and frustration, for it is going to rob me of every single one of my acquisitions in this world.

Indeed, though a person is by nature acquisitive, the very act of acquisition is a source of anxiety, since whatever is acquired can at any moment, and in a hundred different ways, be lost.

I am alone, and yet not alone, for I am together on this planet with trillions of living creatures, all as eager as myself for happiness, all as afraid of pain and sorrow as I am, all presumably with the same right to grasp happiness and flee pain and sorrow to the maximum possible extent. How ought I to relate to these fellow sentient beings in a positive, constructive way?

Life often strikes me as meaningless, as having no more purpose than an idiot's dream; and yet something convinces me that one must somehow make it purposeful in order to be happy and reasonably satisfied. How and where can I find a well defined purpose and meaning?

Our author's answers to these anxieties and questions are explicit. He sees the Buddha Dharma as a means of opening up to every individual who possesses unwavering determination the possibility of integrated development leading to realization of mankind's highest potentialities. In short, a dedicated follower of the essential Dharma teachings can literally become a Buddha, an Enlightened One, in this very life, thus simultaneously actualizing mankind's optimum powers of being, at once alone and with others, in a purposeful and altogether satisfying way.

This book contains no new teaching, but as a restatement of existing teaching, it is magnificent— inspiring!

Unfortunately, the exposition is not intended to be exhaustive, as too much and too varied detail might mar its impact. Hence there are some important omissions such as the operation of karma and the concept of rebirth, both of which are crucial components of the Buddha Dharma. However, the book pioneers a new manner of exposition which can, after all, be employed by the author and/or others to cover the whole range of doctrines comprising the essential Dharma. Guests invited to a copious banquet can hardly complain that the host has set a generous limit on the number of courses. Too much variety at one time can cause serious indigestion.

There is, I believe, just one point on which the author may have gone astray. Near the end of the book he says that the institutionalization of Buddhism led to an idealization of the Buddha that removes him far from man and makes him a shining object of worship, and at the same time makes human beings feel that they are too remote from him to have much chance of closing the gap. I know that many people share this view of one of the Mahāyāna developments, but I think they misapprehend its true significance. I would prefer to state the matter thus:

Theravādins have generally stuck *more or less* closely to viewing the Buddha essentially as a man who realized the utmost potentialities inherent in the human state, so he has remained at the very center of their concept of the Dharma. Mahāyānists, on the other hand, came progressively to center their attention on what might properly be called Bodhi, the potentiality of Enlightenment, viewed as an abstract quality attainable by humans if their determination is firm enough. That Shākyamuni attained Enlightenment in the past is of less significance to them than the fact that Enlightenment is there *now* as a goal to be attained. However, as ordinary people—especially the uneducated masses comprising by far the greater part of the population in the past—find it difficult to conceive of, let alone concentrate upon, an abstract object of worship, this Bodhi principle is often represented by Buddha figures such as Vairocana Buddha, and has been taken at the lower levels of understanding to be a personage. This view, I believe, is confirmed by the huge number of Chinese passages which employ the word *Fo* (Buddha) in contexts where an abstract principle is very clearly intended. Such passages as "The Buddha will be found in your own Mind," or "Fools seek the Buddha and not Mind; wise men seek Mind and not the Buddha" seem to me to make the matter clear.

Well, away with such carping! This excellent book has come to me personally as an illuminating text, despite my close on sixty years' concern with Buddhism. How much more striking must it seem to people with but slight grounding in the Dharma, or none at all!

Bangkok, April, 1982   JOHN BLOFELD

✳

PREFACE

Over the last few years I have become increasingly aware of a crisis in the present condition of Buddhist studies. This situation is characterized on the surface by a polarization into two groups: one consisting of those who follow the approach of the traditional Buddhist schools, and the other of those who approach Buddhism from the standpoint of the Western academic tradition.

In the traditional schools Buddhism is usually portrayed as an historically unconditioned phenomenon that has passed through centuries of time and diverse cultural settings completely unscathed. The teachers of each school claim that their particular tradition represents the 'true', or the 'pure', or the 'highest' doctrine of Buddhism and are often able to cite the scriptures in their favor as well as to trace their lineage back to the Buddha himself. In addition, they insist that Buddhism is a means of salvation and that its real meaning can only be fully realized through integrating its teachings into daily life through the practice of ethics, meditation, and so forth. Thus the traditions emphasize the unchanging character of Buddhism and the necessity of subjective involvement in order to understand it. The Western academic standpoint could not be more different. Buddhism is first of all placed well outside of the observer so that it can be treated with scientific 'objectivity'. It is then subjected to historical and cultural analysis and its scriptures are carefully examined in the light of textual criticism. Any subjective involvement is considered detrimental to the avowed aim of uncovering the objective facts. Hence the prevailing attitude is to consider the manifestations of Buddhism as contingent and transitory phenomena, a true understanding of which can only be gained by observing them from a detached vantage-point.

Between these two poles lies an abyss which, despite the occasional attempts to bridge it, appears as a disconcerting vacuum. But unfortunately, the healing of this split is not just an intellectual problem facing scholars. For, if we go to the heart of the matter, we will find that this apparently external state of affairs mirrors an internal split in the minds of those Westerners who are seriously trying to incorporate the practice of Buddhism into their lives.

The current Western interest in Buddhism as a religion is frequently part of a wider reaction against the confused state of religious, intellectual, and moral values perceived as characteristic of modern Western culture. For many people, particularly the young, the Church appears out of touch with their present situation, and its representatives often suffering from the same doubts and uncertainties that plague everyone else. The intellectual establishment, symbolized more and more by the scientist, seems likewise to be concerned with a reality, which, although fascinating, is for the most part intangible. Moreover, no matter how many findings and advances science makes, it remains, by its very nature, incapable of ever indicating *how* these insights are to be used. So we find ourselves thrust into a situation of moral dilemma and ambiguity where the traditional authority on decision-making vacillates between unbending dogmatism and vague liberalism, while the representatives of science often display considerable uncertainty and divergence of opinion when it comes to ethical issues. Hence the burden of choice comes to rest on the shoulders of political parties and individuals, both of whose better judgement is habitually clouded by self-interest. It is against this background of chaos and contradiction that the spiritual traditions of the East are able to shine out as bastions of wisdom and sanity.

And on closer contact too, that is often how the Eastern traditions appear. The teachers exude a confidence that seems to be rooted in experience rather than fanaticism; the path of spiritual development seems to be clearly mapped; and some of the basic ideas impress one with their apparent compatibility with modern thought. Such an impression, in conjunction with a disillusioned view of Western culture and often a strong psychological need for some kind of certainty in life, enable many people to adopt and finally acquiesce in a traditional form of Buddhism. There is no doubt in my mind that these traditions have a great deal to offer us, but at the same time there are definite dangers involved in accepting them unconditionally. It is all very well to insist on the 'eternal' truth of Buddhism—or any religion for that matter—but one should also realize that it contains numerous relative truths as well. Unfortunately this distinction is frequently overlooked. Moreover, the initial enthusiasm of discovery, together with a fascination for the outward forms of Buddhism, tend to blur the critical faculty. Thus, a situation is created in which what was primarily a response to an existential concern becomes in danger of collapsing into a mere means of escape from one's dilemma. Should this happen (as it frequently does), one finds oneself transposed to an inner world of security— but also of estrangement.

It is simply not possible to uproot ourselves from the soil of Western civilization in which we have grown. No matter how strongly we reject its values, we cannot avoid being a part and product of its development. To turn our attention elsewhere and to absorb ourselves in a foreign religion does not make it go away—it merely relegates it to the shadows. It will inevitably reassert itself: usually in the form of doubts, uncertainties, and an uneasy conscience. To suppress these feelings in the belief that they are negative influences or 'hindrances' to our practice of Buddhism only increases the dangers of fanaticism and further mental unrest. If we are honest with ourselves, we will recognize at this point the need for reconciliation between our Western and Buddhist outlooks. However, at the same time we may also become aware of the considerable distance between them.

Thus we encounter the abyss I mentioned earlier. And when we attempt to bridge it we find precious little help. The traditional teachers of Buddhism as well as the Western academics seem equally determined to hold to their positions so firmly established on either side of the gulf. There are, of course, positive elements and insights present in both approaches, but it is very rare to find them contained in anything approaching a harmonious synthesis. There have been a few attempts to fill this void, but I have found none of them able to offer a fully convincing, satisfying, or creative interpretation of Buddhism that is relevant to the present situation.

This small book is a formulation of my own attempt to come to terms with this 'crisis' both as I have experienced it personally as well as observed it on a more general level. I do not pretend it to be an 'objective' account (if such were ever possible) which only succeeds in reducing the religion to a series of interesting facts about something standing at a comfortable distance from myself. On the contrary, it is a subjective attempt to find words and concepts within my own language and cultural frame of reference capable of satisfactorily articulating my faith in Buddhism. It is spoken from the inside of Buddhism, not from the outside. Through writing down and working out the ideas presented here I am trying to formulate for myself an approach to Buddhism that is compatible with and meaningful within the context of present-day life. As such this work may be of interest to others who are facing the same difficulties as myself in bridging this gulf.

This text is not intended as an exhaustive treatment or interpretation of all the principal concepts of Buddhism. Many of the standard traditional topics, such as the four noble truths, karma, and rebirth, for example, have not been explicity dealt with at all. I am more interested in tracing lines of development rather than extensively detailing the doctrines of any one school. Therefore, I have only chosen certain points that I consider central to the Buddhist path, and have elaborated on them and their interrelations. In this way, the main theme of the book is able to stand out clearly without being obscured by too many peripheral considerations.

The form of the book has come about as the result of a number of different circumstances and conditions. Since 1972 I have been involved in the study of Tibetan Buddhism, particularly of the Gelukpa school, both in India and, more recently, in Switzerland. This training, as well as less extensive studies with other traditions, have provided me with a certain basis in traditional Buddhist thought. Throughout, the central format and themes of this text are strongly influenced by Tsong Khapa's *Great Exposition on the Stages of the Path to Enlightenment* (*lam.rim.chen.mo.*) as well as by Shāntideva's *A Guide to the Bodhisattva's Way of Life* (*Bodhicaryāvatāra*). However, an even greater influence has been the oral explanations I have received to these and other works, which have caused the written words to come alive.

Nevertheless, my increasing difficulty in being able to accept many traditional Buddhist views in the way they are currently presented in the established schools led me to search for a mode of interpretation that would be able to open up the meaning of Buddhism without falling into the extremes of either diluting the original concepts or insisting on a rigid literalism. In order for the Buddhist teachings to resound with the fullness of their meaning, I feel it necessary that they speak to us in a language that we can authentically hear. The presentation of Buddhism in a culturally alien way of thinking often fails to totally communicate the teachings, thereby leaving us existentially untouched.

This search for a coherent means to articulate my understanding of Buddhism led me to the field of modern existentialist philosophy and, in particular, its application to Christian theology. Among the writings of existentialist philosophy, I have found Martin Heidegger's *Being and Time* to be invaluable. Much of the terminology and methodology employed there has been used throughout this book. The influence of existentialist theology has come primarily from Paul Tillich and John MacQuarrie. It has been through their writings that I have become aware of the many possibilities of using existentialist thought as a means of translating and revitalizing traditional religious ideas. In fact, through reading their works I discovered that they, as Christians, were trying to deal with precisely the same problems that I was facing as a Buddhist. Their writings not only gave me many ideas for a means to help resolve these conflicts, but also opened my eyes for the first time to the richness of the Judeo-Christian tradition.

The material in this book started taking shape during 1979 in the form of lecture notes. The manuscript itself was completed in more or less its present form the following year during my stay in the Tibetisches Zentrum, Hamburg.

STEPHEN BATCHELOR
(Gelong Jhampa Thabkay)
Song Kwang Sa, Korea. 1982

"*Every morning the same bright sun rises; every morning there is a rainbow on the waterfall; every evening the highest snowcapped mountain, far, far away, on the very edge of the sky shows with a purple flame; every 'tiny gnat' buzzing around him in the hot sunshine plays its part in that chorus: it knows its place, it loves it and is happy; every blade of grass grows and is happy! Everything has its path, and everything knows its path; it departs with a song and comes back with a song; only he knows nothing, understands nothing, neither men nor sounds, a stranger to everything and an outcast.*"

Dostoyevsky, *The Idiot*

HAVING AND BEING

The more we allow ourselves to be the servants of having, the more we shall let ourselves fall prey to the gnawing anxiety which having involves.

Gabriel Marcel [1]

1. The Dimension of Having

At the very roots of our language we find two verbs: 'to be' and 'to have.' These words have become so absorbed into our unthinking everyday discourse that their primordial meaning has all but been lost. However, they denote two of the most fundamental dimensions of our existence: those of having and being.[2] These two dimensions reveal two distinct attitudes towards life. In terms of having, life is experienced as a horizontal expanse precipitating towards ever receding horizons; in terms of being, life is felt in its vertical depths as awesome, foreboding and silently mysterious. Nowadays, the tendency to be preoccupied with having, at the expense of losing touch with the dimension of being, is becoming ever more pronounced. In times such as ours, when secular and material values dominate social and cultural life to an extreme degree, the intensity of the urge to *have* creates an ever widening gulf from the awareness of who and what we *are*. The primary purpose of Dharma is to reestablish a consciousness of being.

Having is characterized by acquisitiveness. Our worldview is dominated by the notion that the aim of

personal existence is fulfilled in proportion to what we
are able to amass and possess. This craving to acquire
more and more extends into a vast range of different
fields and realms. The most immediate and concrete
realm is that of material objects. We accumulate inanimate things that seem to offer protection, security,
and social status through their tangible and starkly
present solidity.

The other realm is people: husbands, wives, chil-
dren, friends, and acquaintances are all arranged in a
circle around us connected to the center by threads of
attachment and possessiveness. But the scope of having extends even further into the abstract realm of
thought. We have divided this realm into various
fields of knowledge: scientific, political, economic, so-
ciological, historical, religious, and so on, into all the
many subcategories that are constantly emerging. Each
of these fields opens up new possibilities for further
acquisitions. It is symptomatic of our having-oriented
culture that the most intellectually admirable individual is commonly regarded as he who has stored the
greatest number of facts and is able to retrieve them
from his memory in the shortest possible time. Learn-
ing and education have frequently degenerated into
the systematic accumulation of facts and information.
Daily we are confronted with an inordinate quantity of
news and are expected to assimilate it into the stock-
pile of other facts and figures already lying dormant in
our memory. Progress has come to mean the ever increasing ability to accumulate lifeless objects within
the greatest possible number of fields. Aptly we have
dubbed ourselves "the consumer society."

Even our own bodies and minds are regarded as
'things' we 'have.' Life is said to be the most valuable
thing we *possess*. Consequently, body, mind, and life
are all looked upon as objects that 'I' can somehow
keep or lose. Here, as in all acts of having, a gulf is

created between the possessor and the possessed. Having always presupposes a sharply defined dualism between subject and object. The subject thus seeks his or her well-being, as well as his or her sense of meaning and purpose, in the preservation and acquisition of objects from which he or she is necessarily isolated. The maxim becomes: "I am what I have" (Fromm).[2] As a result, any sense of fulfillment will necessarily be illusory, because there is nothing one can *have* that one cannot fear to *lose*. Absorption in the horizontal dimension of having is the origin of all states of ontological insecurity. Anxiety, alienation, loneliness, emptiness, and meaninglessness are the fruits of living as an isolated subject amidst a multitude of lifeless objects. Although our scope of involvement may extend to numerous and diverse fields of interest and concern, as long as the notion of having predominates, our being remains empty and superficial. We wander around as strangers in a 'lonely crowd.'

> We are the hollow men
> We are the stuffed men
> Leaning together
> Headpiece filled with straw. Alas!
> Our dried voices, when
> We whisper together
> Are quiet and meaningless
> As wind in dry grass
> Or rats' feet over broken glass
> In our dry cellar. [3]
>   T. S. Eliot, *The Hollow Men*

What is it that we hope to achieve through all this incessant accumulation? Why are we compulsively motivated to have things? In the first place we instinctively sense that a certain element is lacking in our lives. A vague hunger echoes from deep within us. Perhaps through acquiring material objects, friends, and knowledge this void could be filled. So we set out into the world and start to consume whatever commodities it has to offer. We eat and for a while feel satisfied, but the pangs of hunger always return. Ironically, the more we crave to possess and dominate the world and others, the deeper and more unbearable becomes the chasm of our own emptiness. In order to conceal this rapidly widening gulf our compulsion develops into a frenzy. But, however hard we try, we will never succeed in filling an inner emptiness from the outside; it can only be filled from within. A lack of *being* remains unaffected by a plenitude of *having*.

So habituated are we to dealing with life uniquely within the limits of the horizontal dimension of having, that our consciousness of the possibility of an entirely other dimension of existence, namely, the vertical dimension of being, is rapidly fading to a vanishing point. Consequently, when our quest for fulfillment and meaning turns us to the sphere of religion—the receptacle for the traditional symbols of the dimension of being—we approach it in the only way we know how: as another region of having. Our religion, with its beliefs, rituals, and dogmas becomes another segment among all the other segments that constitute our linear and fragmented existence. It offers us another set of possible acquisitions, even more tempting than all the others: a meaning to life, immortality, enlightenment, the kingdom of heaven. Unfortunately, many organized and institutionalized religions only encourage this attitude. Heaven and hell are emphasized as particular places to which we can go. Enlightenment and eternal life are conceived as things that can be *obtained* by each individual. We can pay for them by accumulating sufficient quantities of the right currency, i.e. merit. Despite the efforts of their founders, the temples continue to be inhabited with those who only sell and buy.[4] In this respect their merchandise has been accurately compared to opium.

The point that cannot be sufficiently emphasized today is that authentic religious consciousness is not another extension of the horizontal dimension of having, but an awakening to the presence of the vertical dimension of being. As such its inception must take place in a radical reorientation of one's entire existence. Similarly, any evaluation or criticism of religion is meaningless when delivered from a horizontal outlook. With the discovery of the dimension of being, the aim and meaning of life is seen within the framework of an entirely new set of values, the principal of which is: *instead of living in order to have more abundantly, it is necessary to live in order to be more abundantly.* Religion should not be considered as an 'optional extra' to life that we can either adopt or discard at will. In its true sense religion is the outcome of life itself. It is not something we adopt in addition to all our other concerns and partition off into a special section of the mind. When firmly rooted in the dimension of being our whole life becomes religious.

Thus the essential dynamic of religion can never be reduced to or identified with a particular system of beliefs or dogmas. Such systematic presentations of the religious essence are inevitable consequences of man's attempt to conceptualize and thereby communicate his experience. As such they are necessary and valuable, but as soon as they arise there is the constant danger that they will be elevated into a set of self-sufficient values existing independently of the deeper reality they attempt to describe. It needs to be constantly borne in mind that all religious institutions and their accompanying belief-systems are culturally and historically conditioned phenomena which point be-

yond themselves to man's ultimate concern. They
themselves are never worthy of such concern; when applied to them it becomes an idolatrous concern.[5]

2. The Buddha's Renunciation

The radical shift from the dimension of having to
that of being, as constitutive of the turning point from
a secular to a religious mode of existence, is dramat-
ically illustrated by the life of Shākyamuni the Buddha. The principal features of the story of his life are
traditionally presented as follows: The Prince Siddhārtha is born as the heir to the throne of Śud-
dhodana, the monarch of the small Shākya kingdom in
Northern India. Shortly after his birth a sage called
Asita predicts that the child will be either a mighty
world ruler or a great religious saviour. Afraid of the
latter alternative his father the King surrounds him
with all variety of sensual pleasures; he is trained for
the kingship, educated, and married. However, he happens to see, on four separate occasions while outside
the royal palace, an old man, a sick man, a dead man,
and a religious mendicant. These events cause him to
ponder more deeply the real meaning of life. Finally,
disillusioned with the vanity of the worldly life, he
secretly leaves the palace one night, discards his
princely garb, dons the robe of a religious mendicant,
and sets out to discover the true purpose of existence.
After several years of practicing various austerities and
meditations under different teachers, he still finds no
answers. Finally, determined to find a solution to his
questions, he sits down alone under a large tree and at
last achieves enlightenment. After some hesitation he
decides to communicate what he has found to mankind and thus embarks on a ministry that lasts for
some forty years.[6]

The value of this account does not lie simply in its attempt to depict historical events, but in its symbolic meaning as a representation of an archetypal process. Although it is presented as the life-story of a particular person set in a particular place and time, its deeper meaning transcends its spatio-temporal horizons. When seen as a description of the transition from the dimension of having to that of being, it can be understood as the original pattern upon which the life of each Buddhist at every time in history can be modeled. This does not mean that in every case its form is to be literally imitated, but that its ontological significance can be realized within each concrete life.

The society into which the Buddha was born offered him two alternative possibilities of existence. On the one hand it was sufficiently stable and affluent to allow a young prince the greatest opportunities to fulfill his worldly ambitions. On the other hand, the political and social organization had developed to the point where men were free to engage in philosophical and religious enquiries concerning the more fundamental meaning and purpose of life. These two alternatives, the former opening into the dimension of having and the latter into the dimension of being, were potentially present from the moment of his birth. Their presence is symbolically disclosed by the prophesy of the sage Asita. However, his father's values clearly lay solely within the scope of having, not in the dimension of being. He lavished all manner of sensual enjoyment upon him, gave him the best education possible, and saw him assure the continuation of the royal line by marrying and producing a son. But all the while he made certain that the painful and negative aspects of life were well concealed from him. Symbolically, the King represents the imposition of the values of a materially oriented secular society upon its individual members.

To this day, those who are firmly entrenched in the horizontal dimension demand that their values remain supreme and unchallenged. This fanaticism is unconsciously motivated by the sense of a vague and indeterminate threat lurking among those inconvenient aberrations of life: aging, sickness, and death. Consequently, these phenomena are concealed in hospitals, homes, morgues and well-tended graveyards. Death and insanity, especially, are even ostracized from speech and, whenever possible, from thought. Anyone who spends his existence dwelling on these things is regarded as 'morbid' or 'unable to enjoy life' and is likewise cast out into the barely tolerated niches reserved for philosophers, monks, and other eccentrics.

However, it was precisely through grasping the significance of old-age, sickness, death, and the life of a religious mendicant that an awareness of the dimension of being arose in the young prince's mind. From this point on his life was radically transformed; he could no longer acquiesce in the superficial values of having and maintain an undisturbed conscience. It would be stretching the imagination too far to suppose that his father's attempts at concealment had caused him to literally have never seen or heard of old-age, sickness, and death. The point is that, in having his attention constantly diverted to possibilities within the sphere of having, he had never realized the deeper existential meaning of these phenomena. From this moment onwards he could no longer be contented with a pursuit of numerous particular achievements, for he was now confronted with the question of the meaning of life as a whole. In the constant shadow of death what real meaning could worldly power and glory have for him? Suddenly all his previous values were declared bankrupt. Instead of seeing the surface of the world as rich and full of meaning, he now perceived it from the deeper vantage-point of being and realized it to be barren and empty. Therefore the real significance of old-age, sickness, and death lies in their function as concrete symbols for the dimension of being. But once they have opened up this dimension, a radically new way of life needs to be adopted that is capable of fulfilling the existential possibilities that have now been revealed. Thus the religious mendicant becomes the living symbol for a mode of existence that seeks life in being as opposed to having.

With this new perspective on life awakening within him the prince began to feel imprisoned in his palace. That is to say, within the confines of the horizontal dimension of having he realized there to be no opportunity for the possibility of discovering the meaning and purpose of being. On four separate occasions he had ventured beyond the boundaries of the 'palace' and had glimpsed the deeper and more fundamental questions of life. These experiences had profoundly disturbed him, but he still returned to the palace and outwardly continued his royal life as before. However, he finally reached a point where the contradiction between the growing intensity of these questions and his superficial life of sensual enjoyment became unbearable. So one night he took leave of his sleeping courtesans and departed from the palace to take up the life of a religious mendicant dedicated to the search for truth. Thus he arrived at a point where a compromise between having and being was no longer acceptable and he had no alternative but to devote himself to a new way of life centered entirely around the principles and values of being. The final departure from the palace, which is also referred to as the 'renunciation,' is thus a symbol for the radical shift from the dimension of having to that of being.

For the following six years he trained himself in the various spiritual disciplines that were practiced in those days but still found no answer to his questions.

Finally he settled down at the foot of the pipal tree and, with the strong determination not to rise again until he had reached his goal, achieved enlightenment and became a Buddha. In the following chapters we shall analyze this process more closely in terms of its ontological and existential significance. We have seen how the renunciation was a description of the shift from the sphere of having to the sphere of being. Likewise the striving for enlightenment can be seen as the process of authentically actualizing the potentialities of human being, and Buddhahood as the actualization of the optimum state of being.

3. The Paradigmatic Character of the Buddha's Life

The more we analyze this account of the Buddha's life, the clearer it should become that its meaning is not restricted to the description of a particular historical event but is of universal significance. It depicts the essential dynamism of Buddhism through the powerful imagery of the life-story of its founder. Thus it synthesizes a description of the process of actualization of the universal potentialities of human existence with the concrete life story of one man. Its true spiritual value lies in its simultaneous portrayal of the personal embodiment of a universal process and the universal significance of a personal life.

Even today each of the main features of the story can be understood in terms of our own personal existence. The 'prophesy' of Asita, as a statement of the innermost existential possibilities into which man can project his being, is just as applicable to us now as it was to the Prince Siddhārtha two and a half thousand years ago. The 'king,' as representative of the values of a having–oriented society imposes his will upon us and conditions the course of our lives in much the same way as he did to the Buddha. The image of the 'palace' is especially powerful today when more and more people are able to surround themselves with sensual enjoyments and material affluence. To an unprecedented degree are old–age, sickness, death, and the religious mendicant kept out of the public view and disregarded by society. Nevertheless, the possibility still remains for us to be struck by the existential questions of life and to make the shift from the dimension of having to that of being. Like the Prince Siddhārtha we may have to secretly slip away form the palace at night while everyone is sleeping. However, this should not be naively interpreted as meaning that it is necessary to actually reject our homes, families, social obligations, and so forth; we can easily do all these things without ever undergoing any radical change within ourselves. The essential element involved in 'renunciation' is our forsaking the *values* of having and awakening to the consciousness of being. We leave behind us "those still sleeping in the palace at night," meaning that we move beyond the condition of ignorantly ('sleeping') and blindly ('at night') indulging in acquisition, possession and consumption ('the palace'), and begin to experience life from a *totally other dimension*.

Genuine renunciation is not a partial or conditional transformation of certain attitudes or beliefs; it involves a radical change of the entire personality. Our very being in the world is transformed. Evidently this process of ontological metamorphosis may effect corresponding changes in our intellectual, emotional, and social behaviour, but any transformations in the latter, no matter how remarkable, are not necessarily indicative of the former having taken place. Moreover, depending on the disposition and circumstances of the individual, this change may occur either suddenly or gradually. However, as is indicated in the story of the

Buddha, it will probably take place over a substantial period of time during which it is nurtured by certain 'key' experiences (by insight into one's mortality, for example) before becoming crystallized in a conscious realization or an overt act. In the following account from the Pali canon the Buddha recalls how this awareness articulated itself in his mind.

> And I too, monks, before awakening, while I was still the *bodhisattva*, not fully awakened, being liable to birth, aging, disease, dying and sorrow because of self, sought what was likewise liable to birth, aging, disease, dying and sorrow. Then it occurred to me, monks: "Why do I, liable to birth, aging, disease, dying and sorrow seek what is likewise liable to these things? Suppose that I, although being liable to birth, aging, disease, dying and sorrow because of self, having known the peril in what is likewise liable to these things, should seek the unborn, the un-aging, the undecaying, the undying, the unsor-rowing, the stainless, uttermost cessation of bondage—*nibbāna*." [7]

This passage, formulated in the language of the earlier adherents of Buddhism, expresses the Buddha's complete change in perspective in terms of a shift in concern from the finite and transient towards the infinite and abiding. Whatever terminology is used the main point remains clear: renunciation involves a total transformation of one's experience of life as a whole.

A point is reached where the contradiction involved in perpetuating a having–oriented existence under the ever darkening shadow of the unrelenting questions of being becomes unbearable. We are left with no choice but to shift the center of our personal life from the dimension of having to that of being. This produces a sense of joyous inner release and freedom from the gnawing uneasiness of our previous vacillation. It is a firm and highly significant transition that is completely irrevocable. We die to the life of external values and are reborn into the life of inner meaning. However, we also find ourselves naked, alone, and homeless. This condition is starkly symbolized by the image of the religous mendicnt, the way of life that the Prince Siddhārtha adopted upon his departure from the palace. It is related how he cut off his hair, exchanged his jewelry and royal clothing for the simple loincloth of a begging monk, and set out alone and homeless in search of the answers to the questions of life. Driven on by his unceasing determination to realize the purpose and meaning of existence he underwent repeated disappointments, extreme physical hardships, and expulsion from even the society of his fellow mendicants. Hence, although the quest for inner meaning may be realized to be the only viable form of existence, it is by no means a life of continuous comfort, ease, and spiritual joy. In accepting this task, we have to constantly confront our deepest anxieties, our emptiness, our despair, our doubts; and there is nowhere for us to escape and hide from them. It is impossible to ever turn back, and at times it seems impossible to ever make any further progress. Within the dimension of being we experience life with greater intensity. In contrast, the values and goals to which we previously gave so much importance are seen to be exceedingly shallow and artificial.

However, Shākyamuni did not become disheartened; he persevered and, through realizing Buddhahood, finally established that an answer was to be found. Thus his life stands as an example which forcibly demonstrates that the inner purpose and meaning of our existence *can* be realized through the process of awakening to Buddhahood. Today, as much as ever before, it presents a direct challenge to each one of us to respond to the deepest questions of our existence in fully actualizing the potentialities of our innermost being.

CHAPTER II

THE TASK OF CLARIFICATION

> *Just as one would examine gold through burning, cutting, and rubbing, so should monks and scholars examine my words. Only thus should they be accepted; but not merely out of respect for me.*
>
> Buddha [1]

4. The Elaboration of the Existential Questions

Through the process of renunciation our personal center moves into a new and unexplored dimension: that of being. The horizontal fields of having do not miraculously disappear: they are there, just as stark and tangible as ever before, but we see them through different eyes. It is as though a barely discernible light has begun to glimmer, the source of which we cannot find. In its glow everything remains exactly the same yet somehow, indefinably, everything is different. This imperceptible transition is illuminating yet highly confusing and even disorienting. We lack a suitable framework within which we can construct a coherent understanding of this dimension. Especially frustrating is the absence of any spatio-temporal perspective and any standard norms of evaluation. By comparison, the well-defined values, laws and institutions founded on the notion of having seem to offer a sound and secure context for living. But having felt the underlying emptiness beneath the pulsations of their mechanisms, we need to seek our means of formulation elsewhere. Thus we are led to the religions of the world that offer us a framework, which claims to describe this new and other dimension, through which man can purposefully express and fulfill his spiritual life.

What is life? How are the potentials of life to be actualized? What is the purpose and meaning of life? These are all questions that gradually formulate themselves in this unstructured region that is slowly disclosing itself to us. They may not, of course, find such explicit expression; they may be felt as a vague but deep anxiety, a sense of disorientation, or a lack of purpose and direction. In any case we are impelled to find a concrete framework in which a set of satisfying answers is provided. The various religions of the world are in fact systematic formulations of the answers to these questions. However, it needs to be constantly borne in mind that these formulations are *formulations for* a particular group of people living in a particular cultural and social milieu at a particular time in history. Therefore, although their essential *content* is determined by universal existential questions, their individual *forms* are determined by the predominant philosophical, cultural, and socio-economic conditions of a particular time and place. A particular religious form or institution retains its validity as a living medium for spiritual experience only as long as its formal determining conditions remain fundamentally unaltered. Once the social and economic conditions, for example, are radically restructured, a corresponding process of restructuring must take place within the formal elements of the religion in order for it to remain alive and vital. This is the task of apologetics: to continually vitalize the original answer (*kerygma*) in the light of the present circumstances, yet without ever subordinating it to them. If the apologetic element is repressed by unbending traditionalism, the religious form begins to ossify until it finally crumbles to dust.

A constant threat to the vitality of religion is the tendency to raise its conceptual and symbolic framework to ultimacy, and then to concern oneself only with its structural forms instead of the inner meaning to which these structural features refer. This trend, together with its destructive consequences, can be clearly seen upon a perusal of the history of most religions. Frequently we find glaring discrepancies between the values and aims of the institutionalized religions and the values propounded and lived by their founders. The latter-day protagonists of the religion become more concerned with justifying and defending the particular dogmas and creeds of their faith, than in grasping their existential significance as answers to the basic dilemmas of human life. The true value of any dogma or belief lies in its ability to point beyond itself to a deeper reality which can not be readily articulated in a simple formula or expression. As soon as its symbolic character of self-transcendence is denied, and the belief is elevated to the status of a final and universally adequate truth *in its own right*, then its genuine spiritual significance is lost, and it is reduced to a mere 'dogma' in the fully pejorative sense of the word. It is important that the symbols and concepts involved in religious belief retain an openness and transparency; all too often they become clouded and opaque, obscuring the very truth they were designed to disclose.

One consequence of this process of formalization and institutionalization is that the religion becomes reabsorbed into the dimension of having. When the concern of its followers is directed solely towards its structural features, it ceases to function as a means of answering the questions implied in existence, and becomes just another receptacle of facts and information. Another consequence of the enshrinement of particular religious forms is that they become increasingly idealized and hence remote from the concrete sphere of human existence. Especially when enframed within the all encompassing context of a developed metaphysical system, they become completely intangible for us mortals due to their supernatural perfection and apotheosis. Hence, in adopting a framework within which to orient ourselves to the dimension of being, we need to be constantly on guard against these tendencies to slip back into the attitudes of having.

What is the meaning and purpose of life in the light of inevitable death? This is an existential question. It requires, and can only be satisfied by, an existential answer, i.e., an answer that responds to the same depths from which the question arose. In order for a religious system to be spiritually meaningful, it must be correlated to the questions which are seeking an answer from it.[2] Moreover, such correlation needs to take into account not only the quality of existential urgency, but also the spirit of the times in which the question is molded. Thus the theological or Buddhist response needs to have as its central issue an answer that corresponds to the central issue of the question, and this answer needs to be expressed in a language that corresponds to the language of the questioner.

Today the principal questions are those of the purpose and meaning of life. For the average man the scientific worldview provides a clear-cut and rational picture of the universe, but it usually fails to account for any underlying aim, purpose, or meaning. This same rationalist and scientific outlook has likewise seriously put into question the validity of the traditional views of the world religions and has thereby undermined the beliefs which previously secured a sense of purposeful existence. Our age is fittingly titled the "space age." The astronaut in his technical and complex machine, effortlessly orbiting the earth, alone and weightless in the emptiness of space, is the perfect symbol of man today.[3] Despite our domination of the forces of nature and our highly developed technology, we have come to feel ourselves as empty, alienated, anxious, and lonely, without any real inner purpose or meaning to our existence. Therefore, to be viable and relevant, the religious answer needs to be constellated around the central themes of purposeful and meaningful existence, and has to be formulated without recourse to supernaturalistic doctrines and speculative metaphysics. It is no solution to naively adopt a belief-structure which was formulated for a different time when man was primarily concerned with the sufferings of embodied existence and salvation in an after-life. The answers of the religions of those times were developed in response to questions which were centered around a different conception of the existential dilemma, and were posed in a language which corresponded to a world view that is no longer feasible.[4] (It is even more absurd to attempt a resuscitation of an anachronistic world view in order to justify one's beliefs). Today the religious answers need to be freshly reformulated *from below,* i.e., in the light of the present existential situation; they can no longer be imposed *from above* as though they were self-sufficient universal truths in themselves.

5. The Answers of Historical Buddhism

The task of Buddhism is to present the truths embodied in it as a meaningful answer to the existential questions that face men and women today. However, in adopting a new form and a more accessible language, it must constantly refer to and be firmly grounded within the traditional trends of Buddhist thought and practice. To remain a Buddhist interpretation it cannot step outside of the Buddhist traditions and attempt to operate independently. It is a question of grasping the significance of the valuable insights of those traditions and reformulating them as solutions to the problems present within contemporary existence. Any criticism needs to be balanced with respect and appreciation.

Within the history of Buddhism two distinct trends in interpreting the significance of the Buddha have been developed. The earlier trend—represented by the Theravāda, for example—is based on a more human and concrete conception of Shākyamuni, whereas the later trend—calling itself the 'Mahāyāna'—developed a more cosmic conception of the founder. These two approaches are centered around the two fundamental attitudes that the human mind adopts in the process of explaining and justifying to itself any phenomenon which is of personal spiritual concern. On the one hand, the being towards whom religious consciousness is focused needs to be accepted as having transcended the limitations of the devotee, but, on the other hand, this being must be sufficiently concrete and human to allow for a fully personal relationship to take place. This paradoxical requirement of a being who is simultaneously concrete and abstract, human and transhuman, is the origin of a great deal of conflict within the history of most of the great religions. In Buddhism this conflict has been polarized into two schools or traditions both of which claim to be either superior or more authentic than the other. Since both poles represent perfectly valid religious sentiments, the conflict will never be resolved through one's managing to completely dominate the other. Its opposite pole will only be temporarily suppressed until the spiritual demands of the human mind forcibly revive it. What is necessary is to attempt a dialectical synthesis, in which the conflicting polarities are resolved in a higher unity.

Throughout the earlier interpretations of Buddhism the concrete and historical figure of Shākyamuni remained as the paradigm of human existence. He was seen as one individual being who, after striving for many lifetimes, finally achieved complete enlightenment, taught the Dharma, and was consummated at death in nirvāna. The goal of his teachings was likewise conceived as the discovery of nirvāna arising as the result of disciplined meditation through which one gains freedom from the processes of com pulsive psycho–physical existence. Although he insisted on compassion and concern for others, these factors were implicitly understood as means whereby to progress to the ultimate goal of nirvāna. Samsāra was conceived as the state of being bound to a miserable and pointless cycle of endless death and rebirth, and nirvāna was seen as its complete antithesis. This completely other condition of freedom could not be described within the categories known to us: it was thus indicated negatively as the 'unborn, unaging, undecaying, undying, and unsorrowing.' Shākyamuni was regarded as the unique historical personage who announced to those bound within samsāra the possibility of nirvāna and the way that leads to its discovery. He offered this salvation within a basically human context, without recourse to any divine intervention or metaphysical speculation. Hence the purpose of existence was to realize through one's own efforts the transcendent dimension of nirvāna and thereby to free oneself from bondage to the transient and unsatisfactory conditions of the world. The Arhat came to embody the goal and aim of human life. Ideally all human activities, either directly or indirectly, were to be focused upon the achievement of his state.

In the later Mahāyāna interpretations the ideal of human life was shifted away from the Arhat towards the Bodhisattva and, ultimately, to the Buddha. As a religious development this movement can be understood as an answer to the call for a fuller focus of spiritual life that embodied the actualization of *all* the essential elements of human existence. As Feuerbach correctly asserted, "To a complete man belong the power of thought, the power of will, and the power of the heart." [5] The Arhat definitely incorporated the perfection of the power of thought as well as the power of will, but his final absorption into nirvāna left him distant and removed from the concrete concerns of the world. It was similar with the human Arhat-conception of Shākyamuni. His love and compassion for mankind were only actually active for forty or so years before he too passed into the inaccessible dimension of nirvāna. It will also be remembered that upon achieving enlightenment he was decidedly hesitant about teaching at all and for several weeks seriously considered passing into nirvāna then and there.

In order that the spiritual needs of man be fully satisfied it is necessary that the objects of his personal striving and faith be the optimal reflections of those very needs. The Arhat—as the aim of one's personal life—failed to provide such spiritual sustenance and inspiration for the total man, and the Buddha—as the object of faith and devotion—was limited by the concrete humanity of Shākyamuni and was no longer reachable in his nirvanic quiescence. In the Mahāyāna conception of Buddhism these two unsatisfied and formless spiritual yearnings were fulfilled by proclaiming the path of the Bodhisattva culminating in Buddhahood, and the cosmic image of the Buddha respectively. In this way a powerful unity was forged between the *striving* to actualize the totality of human life and the *faith* upon which this striving was grounded. The Buddha now came to represent the goal of personal existence as well as its inspirational driving force. Shākyamuni became the concrete historical personage in which the goal of human existence was revealed not only by his explicit teachings but through his very being. The Bodhisattva was conceived as the medium of transition from the state of unfulfilled existence to that of optimally fulfilled existence, namely Buddhahood. Thus the essential feature of the Mahāyāna is that the path and the goal of spiritual life are constantly correlated to the complete existential possibilities contained within the ground. That is to say, the essential human qualities of the powers of thought, will and heart are developed in equal proportion to one another throughout the Bodhisattva path and are finally actualized in equal proportion upon the realization of Buddhahood.

In positing Buddhahood as the final goal and optimum mode of human existence, the Buddha could no longer be considered as simply a superior form of Arhat, who, having taught the Dharma to the world, also passes for ever into nirvāna. The Buddha dwells not in the nirvāna which is the simple antithesis of samsāra but in a nirvāna beyond the extremes of both samsāra and nirvāna. This mode points to the fact that he is free from the bondage and anxiety of samsāra yet fully involved in the fate of those still bound therein. This paradoxical condition of presence/absence could not be contained within the concrete human existence of Shākyamuni; it demanded a more adequate representation. This was supplied by the cosmic notion of the Buddha, in which Buddhahood was conceived as an abiding principle of enlightenment (*dharmakāya*) which transcends yet underlies all its concrete manifestations (*rūpakāya*). Shākyamuni was now seen as a particular—and, in terms of world history, vital—embodiment of this abiding principle.[6]

In this brief description of the development from the earlier to the later understandings of Buddhism, we have concentrated principally on the religious elements, showing how this transition to the Mahāyāna was essentially initiated by an inner demand for fuller possibilities of spiritual expression. However, no phenomenon of human evolution ever takes place in a vacuum; it is always dependent upon a highly complex interrelation of different factors. Hence, to really grasp the meaning of this development, it also should be seen in the light of the prevailing economic, social, and philosophical climate.

Many of the features of Mahāyāna Buddhism were determined by the need to provide a form of Buddhism that was more compatible with the social life emerging out of the political stability found during the Mauryan, Kushan and Gupta empires.[7] This required the molding of a less ascetic image by emphasizing the active and altruistic aspects of the Buddha's life and teachings; a greater attempt at symbiosis with the deeply rooted indigenous Brahmanical culture; and the presentation of the philosophy of Buddhism within a metaphysical format able to hold its own against the competing Hindu systems. This process of adaptation had been gradually gaining momentum ever since the time of Ashoka, as can be seen from certain developments in the Sarvāstavāda and Mahāsamgika schools. In these traditions the concept of the Buddha was becoming more and more transhuman, and the Bodhisattva ideal together with the practice of the perfections was being introduced.[8] But it was not until the first century A.D. that these germinal notions crystallized into the clearly defined and distinct movement of the Mahāyāna. For the following three or four hundred years, throughout the 'golden age' of Indian cultural and philosophial development, the Mahāyāna eclipsed the earlier schools by producing a form of Buddhism far richer in both its metaphysical and devotional elements.

Hence the *content* of Mahāyāna Buddhism was determined by the inner demand for greater spiritual fulfillment within the early Buddhist community, and its *form* was conditioned by the prevailing cultural and philosophical trends current in India during the first centuries A.D. However, certain dangers were present in this attempt to provide a satisfying spiritual and existential solution within an abstract and complex metaphysical framework. On the one hand, under the influence of the indigenous Hindu theology, the introduction of deistic elements brought with it the danger of abstracting the object of existential concern into forms external to oneself. On the other hand, the logical and philosophical concepts, which arose as a result of metaphysical speculation, began to assume a greater importance than the spiritual problems that they were initially designed to solve. The gradual extrapolation of these primarily existential concerns into a religious form, composed of mainly metaphysical concepts, had the ironic consequence of producing a greater sense of alienation between the Buddhist and the Buddha. Although Buddhahood was technically regarded as the optimum development of the essential qualities of man, and, as such, realizable by everyone, by being represented in transhuman, omniscient, omnipresent and divine Buddha figures, there was the constant danger of its becoming conceived as increasingly remote from the sensuous condition of man. The concrete human reality of Shākyamuni was docetically conceived as an ethereal manifestation appearing in a human form. In later speculations even his disciples—including Devadatta—were seen as mere incarnations of distant Buddha figures, and the historical constellation of events surrounding Shākyamuni were regarded as acts of a divine scenario, the real actors remaining carefully hidden behind the scenes.[9] As for the path to Buddhahood, this was extended to encompass inconceivable periods of time—three countless aeons—and thus, as a result of this speculation, man became progressively more insignificant, alienated, and distant in relation to his self-created ideal.

One consequence of this metaphysical development was that the distinctive Buddhist features of the religion were becoming less and less evident—at least to the ordinary lay devotee—and it was gradually reassimilated into the vast fabric of traditional Hinduism. Its influence as an independent movement within India soon declined, and by the 12th century A.D. it no longer had the strength needed to survive the Moslem invasions from the west. Another consequence, however, was the emergence of Tantrism, in India, and Ch'an, in China, as reactions against the current intellectual trends in Buddhism. These were definite existential movements that emphasized the *experience* of the Buddha, and firmly relocated it within the concrete sphere of actual human existence. Both movements affirmed that awakening to Buddhahood was possible in this very life and, consequently, focused upon the Buddha-potential present within each human being as opposed to the alien and remote Buddhas and Bodhisattvas dwelling in their transhuman pantheons. Their rejection of metaphysical interpretation frequently led them to adopt a stance of extreme distrust towards all forms of conceptualization. This resulted in the refusal, or inability, to systematically clarify their position, and thus created the opportunity wherein all forms of vaguely conceived and doctrinally questionable ideas were able to be incorporated into their traditions with little or no resistance. Of course, the existential significance of these movements should not be overlooked because of certain conceptual inconsistencies, but neither should they be unquestioningly elevated to the position of the 'ultimate' teachings of the Buddha. As with all *forms* of Buddhism they are also conditioned by historical and cultural factors and, over the centuries, have succumbed to the ossifying forces of institutionalization and formalism.[10]

6. The Problem of Contemporary Formulation

The solution to our present crisis of trying to understand the inner significance of Buddhism for our own lives today will not be provided by selecting one particular school or tradition of the past and raising it to supremacy over all the others. Such a provincial attitude, which limits itself to one manifestation of Buddhism, has the frequent consequence of causing us to imagine that that form alone represents the true essence of the Buddha's teaching, while every other manifestation is either a propaedeutic for or degeneration from its values and norms. This naturally tends to elevate the chosen historically conditioned tradition into the realm of self-existent spiritual values, and it comes to be worshipped as such. The final and absurd consequence of this attitude is visible today in the modern self-proclaimed champions of anachronistic Buddhist sects righteously and indignantly perpetuating the feuds of their Oriental predecessors in the cosmopolitan settings of Paris, London, and New York. But neither is the answer to be found through dissolving all distinctions into a nebulous eclecticism, in which all ideas, however tenuous their associations, are magnanimously housed under one roof in beatific ignorance of their incompatibilities. Fanatical sectarianism and indeterminate syncretism are simply two extremes, neither of which provides a realistic solution to the problem of integrating the truths of Buddhism into contemporary life.

A historical perspective needs to be maintained

that enables us to be aware of Buddhism as a religion that has undergone much growth and change in its adaptation to different times and places. On occasion its original insights have been revitalized and clarified, at other times it has become overinstitutionalized and subordinated to the prevailing cultural biases. Although deriving its essential characteristics from the life and teachings of the historical Shākyamuni, it is more than a static receptacle of creeds, beliefs, and dogmas that have been faithfully passed down through the ages. It is a living movement of faith, embodied in communities of men and women, that is continuously seeking to express and understand itself. Thus, for a full understanding of its nature it is necesary to be free from attachment to any one historically conditioned form of Buddhism that blinds us to the greater and deeper significance of the whole. This requires a certain 'objectivity'; but not the cold philosophical objectivity of the academic who stands outside the Buddhist faith. A meaningful presentation of Buddhism must be forged out of the struggle of faith to articulate itself.[11] This striving for intelligibility and coherence needs to be grounded in faith, yet it will inevitably be constituted out of the tensions inherent in human religious experience: scripture standing in conflict with interpretation, belief standing in conflict with reason, and tradition standing in conflict with contemporary culture. The aim of this process of articulation is to express the faith in the clearest and most coherent language available without falling into any of the extreme positions, i.e. literalism or fundamentalism, on the one hand, or liberalism or positivism, on the other.[12] A valid and relevant Buddhist understanding needs to emerge in dialectical dependence upon these various elements. With this consideration in mind it should be clear that *no particular interpretation or expression of Buddhism can ever be final.*

Buddhism, just like any other phenomenon, is a depen-
dent-arising and therefore lacks an inherent self-na-
ture. Unfortunately, this insight of Nāgārjuna has
rarely been applied to the very body that proclaims it.

Once we have recognized the relative nature of all
the various schools and trends within Buddhism we
need not focus on their mutual conflicts and disagree-
ments. Our aim is to evaluate their insights in the light
of the present situation and to disclose the *existential*
significance of Buddhism, since it is precisely this aspect which is the most relevant to man's situation today. As a conceptual framework we can here adopt
some of the terminology of modern existentialist
thought and make use of its phenomenological methodology. The advantages of interpreting the traditional doctrines of Buddhism in such a way are twofold: on the one hand we may be able to see more
clearly certain concepts that are concealed from us by
a language and way of thinking that belong to a culturally alien and historically distant world view, and on
the other hand we may reach a better understanding of
the ontological structures and possibilities of man that
are implied within the Buddhist teachings upon which
the practice of Buddhism is enabled to unfold. An existential model is particularly appropriate in that it is
able to acknowledge the strong existential character of
Buddhism and at the same time address itself to the
existential crises that technological man is confronted
with today. It provides a valuable point of encounter
where Buddhism and modern man can authentically
meet one another while still retaining their individual
distinctness. At present one is usually sacrificed to the
demands of the other: either Buddhism is only partially accepted (e.g., as a meditation technique), or it is
watered down so as to be compatible with certain
modern prejudices, or the insights of contemporary
culture (e.g., the natural sciences) are unthinkingly dis-

carded in order to embrace an archaic view of the world that seems to be demanded by Buddhist faith. By centering our attention upon existential concerns we can delineate the dimensions of human life to which Buddhism directly applies and thus be in a better position to evaluate its relation to the other disciplines.

Our present situation is fundamentally similar to that of the prince Siddhārtha. In both cases life has come to be dominated by the unrelenting forces of material and secular values. The concern of man is utterly absorbed and lost in the depersonalized mass of particular entities in the world. In both cases an existential reaction, motivated by a deeper and more compelling awareness of the question of life as a whole, has arisen. The story of the Buddha indicates that his seeing an old man, a sick man, a corpse, and a wandering mendicant, impelled him to renounce his palatial life. This reaction is evident nowadays in the questioning of our basic values, our notion of progress, and our attitude towards technology. It reveals itself in Kierkegaard's study of anxiety, Marx's concern with alienation, Heidegger's analysis of inauthenticity and death. It is expressed throughout modern literature in the terrifying imagery of Kafka, the despair of Eliot, and the nauseating pointlessness of life described by Sartre. In this light, the 'awakening' of the Buddha should be seen as the actualization of a meaningful answer to the questions implied within existence, and the teachings of Buddhism as a description of the processes involved in the realization of authentic life. Although the traditional schools of Buddhism have often lost themselves in considerations of their formal and structural intricacies, there remain visible in all of them basic existential insights that further clarify the nature of the Buddhist experience. It is these elements that need to be identified and brought to prominence here. It is important that we try to avoid any sectarian bias—Hīnayāna vs. Mahāyāna, etc.—and seek to disclose the underlying existential and ontological significance of the doctrines of the different schools. We may thus succeed in preserving the essential insights of Buddhism into the nature of man and his way to awakening that have been developed throughout its history, without ascribing superiority to any one insight and the school that has grown up around it.

CHAPTER III

BEING-ALONE

The answers implied in the event of revelation are meaningful only in so far as they are in correlation with questions concerning the whole of our existence.

Paul Tillich [1]

7. The Phenomenological Approach

Before we can more fully understand the structures of the Buddhist path, it is necessary that we clearly grasp the basic elements of man's being upon which those structures are founded. More precisely, we need to recognize those fundamental constituents of man's being that are themselves authenticated through the process of the path. The practice of Buddhism is not concerned with the erection of a superstructure upon a set of passive data which remain unchanged, but with the transformation of life itself from a state of disorder and chaos into a condition of wholeness and purposefulness. A 'transformation' implies that *something* undergoes a process of change or restructuring. The clearer we can initially describe and ascertain this 'something,' the more firmly based will our subsequent analyses of the Buddhist path be. Because this is a phenomenological approach, we must attempt to temporarily suspend our habitual judgment patterns and allow ourselves to confront the 'phenomena' as they disclose themselves to us.[2] It is valuable in that we are able to gain a grounding in the structures of our own existence from where to determine the degree of ontological correlation present in the particular doctrines of Buddhism. It is tentative and preliminary since in practice a complete suspension of judgment is rarely possible. For this reason, whatever understanding we reach by this approach will need to be continually revised and reevaluated in the light of further experience.

Every teaching of Buddhism contains certain ontological presuppositions. Implicit within each individual doctrine and statement is an underlying view of man in terms of his ontological constitution and possibilities . When it is said that "the cause of suffering is craving," for example, in addition to making an explicit assertion about a causal relationship between two evident features of man's existence, a tacit understanding of the underlying structure of man is assumed.[3] It is implied that man is a being in whose very being there dwells the possibility to crave and to suffer. The ability to crave likewise implies that the being of man is such that he can be concerned with entities other than himself. By analyzing the various statements of Buddhism in this way a picture can be gradually constructed of the Buddhist view of man's being. And it is this implicit ontological model that needs to be evaluated in the light of phenomenological description. With this methodology we are enabled to clarify the compatibility of the Buddhist teachings with the actual structures of human existence. We are thus in a position to distinguish between those insights grounded in an experiential awareness of man's being and those doctrines which are based on mere intellectual speculation or over–literalist interpretation. It is important that every possibility of being is established as a genuine possibility rooted in the actual structures of man's existence, and is not just wishful thinking which, although perhaps logically deducible from certain statements, is no longer existentially founded.

Our enquiry here is based on the ontological structures of man's being-alone and being-with.[4] These fundamental elements are revealed in the paradoxical characteristic of existence of always finding ourselves inescapably *alone* and at the same time inescapably together in a world *with* others. They stand in a relation of simultaneous polarity and interdependence. That is to say, they are opposing poles of man's existence, yet at the same time they are bound-up in an inseparable unity. Our sense of aloneness and individuality is only conceivable in the light of our constant coexistence with other human beings, and we can only be together with others and participate in their lives because we and all others are in fact distinct individuals. Distinction is a necessary component of the unity found in all relationships.

The nature of these two elements, aloneness and participation, as fundamentally constitutive of man's being needs clarification before we can consider them in the light of the insights of the Buddhist path and, at the same time, see whether insight into them helps, in turn, to illuminate the nature of that path. At present we are subjected to a constant tension between these poles. At times an inclination to individuality at the cost of participation disrupts our existence, and at times our individuality is threatened with dissolution through submission, imposed or voluntary, to the will of another or to the force of an impersonal collective. As long as we remain human beings, it is impossible for either pole of this polarity to be entirely reduced to the other. The being of man would be irretrievably broken down and no longer recognizable as human were such a dissolution to take place. There are, however, varying degrees of existential disruption which result from the tension between these poles.[5] Moreover, each of these poles represents a region of possibility that is constantly being actualized in our thoughts, words and actions. For the most part, however, this process of actualization is *inauthentic*. By 'inauthentic' it is meant that the actualization of the full range of possibility within either one's being-alone, or being-with is avoided and becomes limited. In the case of being-alone, we will see that such actualization of possibility is limited by ignorance and selfishness; in the case of being-with, by self-concern and disregard for others. Thus in correlation with these two poles of existence, two distinct modes of inauthenticity become evident: inauthentic being-for-oneself and inauthentic being-with-others. In contrast, the Buddhist path is a means of overcoming this inauthenticity and of fully realizing both authentic being-for-oneself and authentic being-for-others.

8. Aloneness and Anxiety

Our fundamental aloneness is disclosed to us through our birth and more strikingly through our death. Shāntideva starkly presents this insight in his words, "At birth I was born alone, and at death too I shall die alone." [6] At birth we are choicelessly thrown into an existence which is exclusively our own. This existence rests in a stubborn facticity which irresistibly opens ahead into a future which holds only one certainty, death. Ontologically, 'birth' should not be restricted to denoting the physical act of being born, but needs to be understood as our ever-present rootedness in the given and inalterable structures of our past. This is what is meant by the term 'facticity.'[7] Furthermore, one's facticity is disclosed to oneself alone and cannot be shared with others. It is in solitude that we are constantly confronted with our having-been-born. This awareness may rarely be conceptually formulated, but it is always present as a fundamental mode of the way in which we find ourselves in the world.

Our being inescapably grounded in a set of predetermined structures always lies behind us, so to speak, but we are rarely consciously concerned with these, instead our existence is constantly directed ahead into an indeterminate future. What lies ahead is revealed to us through our being confronted with possibilities. Our possibilities, however, are not unconditional and infinite but are limited by the structure of our actual existence. Nevertheless, within the range of possibilities open to us we are free to be actively concerned with the choices and decisions that will determine the future. Thus the choices we make are only free "in the sense that they are not infallibly predictable from the conditions in which they are made, not in their being absolutely unconditioned." [8] Our lives are, therefore, constituted within the framework of another polarity: that of facticity and possibility. Our existence is stretched between them in tension. We always stand between an inescapable 'given' and an inescapable 'ungiven.' Sartre neatly sums this up in his expression, "Man is condemned to be free." [9]

Although the future stands before us in its uncertainty, this *uncertainty* will be paradoxically and finally curtailed by the utter certainty of death.[10] In the words of Heidegger, "death is the possibility of the absolute impossibility" of man's existence.[11] Death is not, as we usually conceive it, merely an event that will just happen sometime; it is an everpresent possibility in the face of which our actions, either consciously or unconsciously, are to some degree determined. The tension between facticity and possibility is thus further compounded by death, which is the only possibility within our given human existence that is impossible to avoid. Its absolute inevitability indicates that it is fundamentally constitutive of life. Life unrelentlessly moves towards death, towards that moment, perhaps today, perhaps in many years hence, when everything in this world will conclusively stop for us. Moreover, we face our death in utmost solitude. In the moments when this overwhelming possibility vibrates through us, we become acutely and uneasily conscious of our aloneness, insignificance, and helplessness. It is no use dismissing such thinking as morbid and pessimistic: the fact of death is ineluctably present, and it has to be taken into full account in any view of man.

All this serves to describe the very foundations that underlie our being-in-the-world. We are trying to glimpse—with the help of Heidegger's analysis—the ontological bases from which our thinking, feeling, and acting arise and are possible. Within the scope of aloneness our existence is suspended, as it were, in the space of possibility between birth and death, which, in turn, were preceded and will be followed by the impenetrable. This is the condition we dimly yet deeply are faced with as long as we live. But our role is not that of passive spectators; we are *thrown* into existence and its possibilities are *thrust* upon us. We constantly are confronted with a future that irretrievably plunges to the past, but in doing so demands that we firmly seize it in the present moment and *project* our possibilities into actuality. Therefore at origin, our thoughts and deeds are responses to our sheer being in the world. They are attempts to make sense of the overpowering incomprehensibility of existence, they are efforts to find happiness and security in its alien and threatening presence.

Man is faced with the task of being responsible for his existence. His being-in-the-world is primordially disclosed to his concern. But under the menacing and inescapable shadow of death, existence as such is anxiously felt as too massive and overwhelming to be concernfully accepted in its totality. Consequently we shy away from the immensity of being and the imminence of death and fall into a preoccupation with particular entities within the world.[12] In this way we flee from our essential being into the illusory security offered by external situations composed of discrete things. Our concern becomes that of manipulating and organizing entities in such a way that finally, so we hope, our anxieties and fears will be able to come to rest in an utterly secure world. We justify all such activity by appealing to the authority of 'them,' the public, the crowd.[13] But in doing so we lose our very selves, and our voices become just further stereotyped echoes of what everyone else thinks and says, in short, we become absorbed in the dimension of having.

This flight from our existential responsibility into absorption with particular entities is a basic characteristic of inauthentic being–alone. It illustrates a fundamental trait of the condition of samsāra. The root of this condition is a state of ignorance [14] in which we are blind to being itself and are only conscious of particular entities.[15] Moreover, this state of ignorance ascribes an inherent self–sufficiency to the entities with which it is concerned and thus raises them to an illusory position of ultimacy. Oneself, others, things in the world, as well as the world itself, are instinctively regarded as bearing their own discrete self–existence without depending upon any other causally conditioning factors or component elements. We subsequently find ourselves in a world composed of numerous finite entities standing alone and essentialy unrelated. This situation seems to offer us security, predictability, and manageability. Here we can safely concern ourselves with things that are fixed within definite boundaries, and thereby avoid being concerned with the troublesome incomprehensibility of our existence as a whole. Unfortunately, however, our flight into samsāra provides only an illusory sense of security and well–being. However hard we try to convince ourselves that all is well and that there is really nothing to worry about, we cannot prevent the underlying tensions of our existence from occasionally erupting to the surface and shattering our complacency.

In these moments we experience *anxiety*. Anxiety is quite different from fear, which always has as its object a particular entity within the world, and can thus be dispelled through either removing the object or removing oneself from the object.[16] Anxiety is not focused upon any particular entity, but upon our existence as such. "That in the face of which we have anxiety is thrown Being-in-the-world; that which we have anxiety about is our potentiality-for-being-in-the-world." [17] In anxiety we are confronted with the overwhelming fact of our having been born alone and our having to face inevitable death alone. That which we sought to evade by fleeing into the domain of particular entities is all of a sudden starkly and manifestly present in all its immensity. It produces anxiety because it threatens the very core of the supposed security and meaningfulness we like to believe we have found in the world of things. Such ontological anxiety can be highly disturbing because in its grip we realize that our whole lives have been spent in restless pursuit of distant shadows and phantoms while that which is the closest to us, our very existence, has been ignored. We come face to face with the disconcerting fact that our absorption in the realm of particular things is a senseless and hopeless flight from something we can never escape. However much we try to brush aside anxiety, dismiss it as irrational or neurotic, and forget its content by returning to the more pressing concerns of the world, death will never go away.

We are reminded here of Prince Siddhārtha who, although surrounded by all the material wealth and sensual pleasures he could wish for, was deeply disillusioned with the palace life. His father had tried his best to keep him hidden from the underlying conditions of existence, but the Prince had happened to see, while outside the palace, an old man, a sick man, a corpse and a wandering mendicant. These events produced within him a vivid awareness of his ontological constitution of being thrown into the world and having to die. He was now confronted with his existence as such which he had previously avoided through absorption in the realm of particular entities. He had justified this by submitting to the identity imposed upon him by 'them,' the public (who, in the story, are symbolized by the king). Now that the illusion of security in the world of things was dispelled and he realized the extent of his existential responsibility, he experienced a deep anxiety. "Though the son of the Shākya king was thus tempted by priceless objects of sense, he felt no security, he found no contentment, *like a lion pierced deeply in the heart by a poisoned arrow.*" [18] It was this state of anxiety that forced him to renounce the world, whose values were focused solely in the domain of particular entities, in order to accept his existence in its totality and penetrate to its inner meaning.

In looking back we can see that two levels of anxiety are involved. The first, which for the most part is inarticulate and instinctive, drives man into his concernful absorption with the world of particular things. The second is far more critical and desperate, since it is based upon and incorporates the realization that absorption in such a world is unable to provide a secure retreat from the responsibility of facing one's existence in its totality. The fundamental anxiety that motivates our flight into the world is temporarily removed through the hope that the objects and situations of the world will provide us with a final refuge. When this hope is dashed through the discovery that such a refuge is illusory, our original anxiety is inevitably heightened and intensified. In addition we now experience acute despair, hopelessness and emptiness. Such deep and fundamental anxiety may only be felt for a moment or two before we hastily cover it up with our habitual rationalization and chatter. But as long as we remain lost and absorbed in the domain of particular entities, we are constantly subjected to its unpredictable irruption. Again, as Heidegger says, "Anxiety is there. It is only sleeping. Its breath quivers perpetually through man's being." [19]

For some people, perhaps for the majority, states of anxiety may be restricted to the periphery of their existence and dismissed as passing moods. For others, however, the significance of anxiety in disclosing a fundamental insight into human existence is grasped. At this point their consciences will never allow them to return to a contented absorption in particular entities. Any such attempt to do so will be felt deep down as a betrayal of their truer instincts. Those things which previously were experienced with full satisfaction will now seem shallow, hollow, and somehow meaningless. We come to understand with greater and greater clarity that absorption in the world of things provides no refuge, and one ceases to center one's hope in them. At this critical juncture of human existence two basic alternatives remain: either to dismiss existence in general and man's existence in particular as essentially futile and absurd, or to place one's hope in the actualization of a greater purpose or meaning that is not immediately evident within the realm of empirical data. It is questionable whether the first of these alternatives, if strictly followed through, could in practice provide a sufficient basis for a genuinely human existence. It seems that a certain element of hope is necessary for any human life to effectively continue.

The second alternative is one in which the aim of our lives becomes the achievement of a goal that claims to bring to actualization the fullest extent of our human potential. Such goals, as well as the paths of thought and action inspired by them, are various and diverse, ranging from the communist utopia of Marxism, to the Christian Kingdom of Heaven, and the Nirvāna of Buddhism. Here we concentrate mainly on clarifying the paths and goals of Buddhism.

9. *Taking Refuge*

In accepting what is revealed by anxiety as existentially significant, we experience disillusionment with the security offered by particular objects and situations, and are freshly confronted with the sheer fact of our existence. We have no choice but to directly face this fact without succumbing to the temptation of covering it up again in evasion and flight. We need to grasp in its entirety the ontological conditions of facticity and possibility disclosed to us and, in doing so, come to accept our radical aloneness, finitude and disruption. In these moments of anxious acceptance we are able to perceive, perhaps only dimly and fleetingly, the phenomenon of our being at all, rather than not being. However, this being is not static and passive; it is a dynamic becoming grounded in facticity and opening ahead into possibility. As such it stands before us as the prearticulate question: "to what end?" Existentially, the teleological question is prior to any aetiological questions. That is to say, the *purpose* of our existence is of living and vital concern since we are constantly moving ahead into its potential actualization, whereas the *causes* of our being lie in the realm of the factically given and are no longer a possibility for us. With this fundamental question of the purpose and meaning of our life anxiously resounding within us, we are compelled to find an answer that resounds with comparable depth and hope.

The pre-articulate question is posed to us originally not conceptually but ontologically, i.e. our very being becomes a question for us. The explicit formulation of this question in such forms as, "What is the purpose of existence?" or, "What is the meaning of life?" is a subsequent articulation referring to a pre-articulate state of being. As with all articulate sounds these forms of the question are necessarily referential.[20] Indeed, how could any questions ever cause us existential concern without our first becoming aware of them within the constitution of existence itself? The danger here is that we tend to identify the ontological question with its conceptual reflection and then set about to seek the answer in similar conceptual terms. This is an unrealistic pursuit. The explicit question, "What is the meaning of life?," will never be satisfactorily answered by another sentence, "The meaning of life is x, y, z." Judged as an articulate question it can be said to have little or no significance. It is only when the question ceases to be identified with the subject–verb–predicate structure of grammar, and is recognized within its original ground, within existence itself, that we can start looking for an answer. But such an answer will not be restricted to the confinements of language; it too must be revealed within an existential structure. Moreover, to be fully meaningful it must correlate directly with the structure of the question. And since the question— the life of man—is human in structure, likewise the answer too must be revealed in a human structure.

For a Buddhist the answer to the questions implied within existence is the Buddha himself. It is the very life of Buddha Shākyamuni—his renunciation, his enlightenment, and his active participation in the life of other men—that provides an existential answer to man's existential questions. Being a Buddhist is not merely determined by the acceptance of certain beliefs and the rejection of others. The essence of Buddhist faith resides in an ontological commitment that is prior to all articulate formulations. This commitment consists of a concernful recognition of Buddhahood as an answer to man's existential questions, and a hopeful redirecting of one's life towards that mode of being. It is the forging of an ontological bond between our present state of human facticity and its optimum possibility.[21] Our being as disclosed to us in anxiety reaches forth in its totality to the hope of fulfillment and meaningfulness as manifested in the Buddha. Hence this commitment is a movement that takes place deep within us; it is not merely a change–over from one set of beliefs to another. In the same way as the articulation of the existential question is a conceptual reflection of a deeper concern, so is the intellectual formulation of a set of beliefs a conceptual reflection of the concernful acceptance of the existential answer. It is when this level of deeper prearticulate concern is ignored or forgotten, and metaphysical speculation, creeds, organized sects, and elaborate rituals assume primary importance, that the danger of a religion's falling prey to secular, having–oriented interests arises. For Buddhism to remain fully alive and valid its existential dimension needs to be constantly emphasized.

It is the two factors, anxiety and hope, that constitute the essential dynamic of 'taking refuge.' [22] Anxiety is the cause for seeking refuge, and hope is the essence of taking refuge. Habitually, as we anxiously flee from the responsibility of our existence as a whole, we place our hope in the particular objects and situations of the world. This, however, fails to provide us with a secure refuge and our initial anxiety asserts itself again. Now we take refuge in Buddha. The difference here is very great. Whereas formerly we sought to *avoid* facing up to our being, here we fully *accept* our being and hope to actualize all its potentialities in the optimum state of being revealed in the Buddha. It is only through radical acceptance of what we are, and the adoption of a path that takes into account the

unfolding of our totality, that anxiety can be transcended and finally overcome. Here we come upon one
of the most distinctive features of Buddhism, namely
the fact that Buddha does not represent a transhuman
absolute value, but stands for the optimum mode of
being that man himself is capable of realizing. The
Jataka literature, in particular, serves to illustrate very
clearly that Shākyamuni *became* a Buddha by gradually bringing to fulfillment his own potential. Factically, man is prior to Buddha.

It is important to recognize that refuge is not
sought in Shākyamuni but in Buddha. Buddha represents a mode of being that historically was actualized
by Shākyamuni, and was then articulated to man
through the words and deeds of Shākyamuni and his
followers. Each significant development in the history
of the Buddhist community emerged simply through
further insight being gained into the nature of Buddha, and this then being coherently expressed to the
community in the best available concepts of that time.
As we have already seen, in the early community emphasis was laid upon the enlightenment and nirvanic
freedom discovered by Shākyamuni, whereas in the
later community more importance was given to his altruistic participation in the world of men and his transcendence of quietism. In each case light was being
shed on different facets of the essential constitution of
Buddha as the community strove to understand the
inner nature of the existential answer to its anxiety.

However, refuge is not sought in Buddha alone,
but in the three Jewels: Buddha, Dharma, and Sangha.
Although Buddha remains throughout as the central
principle of refuge, here the character of that refuge is
refracted into three in order to cover the entire relationship between man in his present samsaric condition and man's optimum mode of being.[23] Refuge in
Buddha pertains to the cause as well as the result of

the process of authentication. As manifested historically in Shākyamuni, for example, a paradigm of authentic human existence is revealed; through his words and deeds he provides a focal point of inspiration and guidance for others. The 'causal' aspect in the Buddha refuge is the guidance that reveals and initiates the process of authentication. The 'resultant' aspect of the Buddha refuge is the optimum mode of being—Buddhahood—that stands as the end result of that process. Thus the Buddha represents the dynamic unity of these two elements: his active participation in the world being the visible expression of his entire being. Dharma refers to the process of authentication itself. This likewise has two aspects: 'paths' and 'cessations.' The paths include all the stages of development involved in moving from our present state of disruption to a fully authentic state of being, and the cessations constitute the final transcendence of distorted modes of being. The term 'Dharma' is also used to denote the teachings and instructions Shākyamuni and his followers gave concerning the actualization of this process of development. However, as a refuge, the principal significance of Dharma is that of its being the process of authentication itself. Finally, the Sangha is the community of faith that provides the supportive condition necessary for the effective actualization of Dharma. It is comprised of those individuals who have accepted the Buddha as the answer to their existential predicament and are engaged in resolving the tensions and disruptions of their existence through redirecting their lives along the paths of Dharma that lead to the Buddha's mode of being. Therefore, in taking refuge in the three Jewels we turn away from all samsaric concerns and strive to fundamentally restructure our lives around the principles of Buddha, Dharma, and Sangha.

Essentially, the taking of refuge is centered around

the radical shift from concern with particular entities
to concern with fulfilling the possibilities of the totality of one's being in the actualization of Buddhahood.
This corresponds to the shift from the dimension of
having to the dimension of being. While we have hitherto concentrated on formulating the Buddhist answer
to the conflicts involved within the region of man's
aloneness, we have not yet taken into sufficient account the equally important aspect of his participation
in the world with others. It is to this area of man's
being and to the disruption and inauthenticity present
therein, that we shall now turn our attention, and attempt to clarify the Buddhist approach to an authentic being-with-others.

CHAPTER IV

BEING-WITH

As Being-with, man 'is' essentially for the sake of others . . . Even if the particular factical human being does not turn to others, and supposes that he has no need of them or manages to get along without them, he is in the way of Being-with.

Martin Heidegger [1]

10. The Ontological Ground of Participation

Not only are we inescapably alone in the realms of our private thoughts, perceptions and feelings, but we are also, paradoxically, inescapably together in a world *with* others. This should not be interpreted superficially as simply meaning that each individual lives in and shares a world with numerous other individuals in a way similar to one tree standing side by side with countless other trees. In its essence being-with-others is not a spatial but an *ontological* relation. This is to say, our coexistence with others is not merely accidental, i.e. something which could equally well *not* be the case, but is fundamentally constitutive of the very way we are. Even when we are physically alone and experiencing loneliness we are still essentially with others; indeed, the very fact that we can feel lonely indicates that participation is a basic structural element of our being. Loneliness is not only positively characterized by a certain degree of isolation, but is negatively characterized by a deficiency of participation.[2] Thus, as soon as we come into existence, we are inextricably bound together with others. However, we are not bound together from the *outside*, by external factors that happen to bring us into contact, but from the inside, by the essential constitution of our being.

Two factors in particular serve to illustrate the deep structural presence within us of being-with-others: thought and speech. These phenomena are likewise inseparably related: we silently think to ourselves in the language we speak, and in speaking we vocalize our thoughts to others. Although thoughts only take place in the inaccessible sphere of our aloneness, their very occurrence is a constant witness to the presence of others. On the one hand, the words and ideas in which we think are only meaningful within the trans-individual context of a common linguistic framework. On the other hand, the inner aim of thought is never fully realized until it ripens into vocal utterances through which others can have access—albeit indirect—to our personal experience. In fact, an inner experience only achieves true completeness when it has been *spoken*.[3] No matter how profound an insight one may gain, as long as it stays inarticulately concealed within an introspective silence, it remains one-dimensional and incomplete. However inadequate our words and concepts may be in accurately communicating our experiences, it is only in the act of conceptualizing them to ourselves and subsequently articulating them to others that they finally come to completeness. Only through articulation can an inner experience realize a degree of dimensional complexity that fully harmonizes with our ontological constitution. Genuine understanding, whether of an external state of affairs or of ourselves, is guaranteed neither by the inexpressible quality of a private perception nor by the clarity of a conceptual formulation. Genuine understanding is a state of a higher dialectical unity grounded in, yet irreducible to, either of these two poles.

Thus language, whether spoken quietly to ourselves

or out loud to others, because of the essential role it plays in our lives, is the most immediate proof of the inescapable being-with-others that pervades our existence. Thought and speech are only conceivable in a being who is essentially with others. Moreover, it is worthwhile to note that in both the Hellenic and Buddhist traditions language, i.e., thought and speech, is regarded not as a secondary but as a defining characteristic of man. In classical Greek thought man is defined as "the living being having the capacity for discourse," whereas the popular Buddhist definition reads, "the being who speaks and understands meanings." [4] Since language is only possible for one who is essentially with others, these definitions strongly imply that being-with lies at the core of man's being and not on the periphery. This being the case, we can no longer consider as complete a view of man's development that fails to take sufficient account of man's being-with-others. Indeed, if we accept the foregoing analysis, it would seem that *primary* importance should be attached to the fulfillment of our capacity to be with others, since it is this potential—in its most evolved form as language—that defines man. In the light of these considerations a major oversight can be detected in those who disparage thoughts, ideas, and words as 'mere intellectualizations' that obscure reality. In rejecting the development of thought, they thereby reduce their capacity to develop authentic being-with-others, and subsequently are liable to embark on a path of one-dimensional spirituality.

It was the growing awareness of the ontological significance of man's being-with-others that formed the basis for the gradual emergence of the so-called 'Mahāyāna' developments within the Buddhist community. By the time these movements crystallized into clearly defined traditions, during the early centuries A.D., the shift of emphasis away from the Arhat ideal to the Bodhisattva had resulted in a complete reorientation of direction. As a somewhat extreme example of this divergence let us compare the following two statements. In the *Dhammapada*, one of the earliest popular anthologies of Buddhism, we read, "Because of others' welfare, however great, one's own welfare should not be neglected. Well perceiving one's own welfare, be zealous regarding self-interest." [5] Whereas, several centuries later, Shāntideva writes, "Upon realizing the faults of self and the ocean of good in others, one should completely reject all selfishness and accustom oneself to accepting others." [6] What could occasion such a fundamental shift in a community's attitude other than an equally fundamental reevaluation of the essential structure of man's being? Although the *form* of Mahāyāna Buddhism was conditioned by the prevailing cultural and philosophical trends current in India during the first centuries A.D., its *content* was determined by the inner demand for greater spiritual fulfillment. This 'inner demand' refers of course to the deeply felt need to fully integrate into religious life the essential human characteristic of being-with-others.

However plausible the above interpretation may be, the attempt to explain a particular historical development within Buddhism in the terminology of modern ontology might appear to be unjustified because of its introduction of concepts from an entirely non-Buddhist secular discipline. What doctrines, we may ask, are there within the Buddhist tradition itself to justify the use of such concepts? First of all, we must remember that ontological concepts such as 'being-with-others' are only *implicitly* contained in most traditional religious thinking, and are subsequently brought to light by phenomenological analysis. However, within Mahayanist literature there are very strong grounds for supposing a deep prearticulate awareness of being-with-others as the underlying theme behind many of its explicit doctrines. For example, the seminal notions of an 'awakening mind,' 'method,' and the 'form body' are evidently founded on an awareness of the need to incorporate one's essential relatedness with others into the core of spiritual life.[7]

Perhaps the closest any Buddhist writer comes to formulating a concept similar to 'being-with-others' is Shāntideva in his *Bodhicaryāvatāra* where he discusses the equality of self and other and the exchange of self for other.[8] In one passage he asks himself, "In the same way as the hands and so forth are regarded as limbs of the body, likewise why are embodied creatures not regarded as limbs of life?" [9] Thus he affirms, by means of this analogy, a natural inner unity and relatedness between living beings. Elsewhere, by referring to the same analogy, he illustrates how self-centeredness is a distortion of this basic unity and thus, in ontological language, an inauthentic being-with-others. He makes this point in dealing with the objection that suffering should only be attended to by the being who is actually experiencing it. To this he replies, "But the suffering of the foot is not that of the hand. Why then does it protect it?" [10] In this way, through appealing to the inherent inner unity between beings, which we have referred to as 'being-with-others,' he points to the inescapable necessity of integrating this element into spiritual life and thereby authenticating it.

11. Inauthentic Being-With-Others.

Although being-with-others is a fundamental characteristic of the way we are, in our actual attitudes towards and behaviour with others it assumes one of two manifest modes: it is either authentically or inauthentically fulfilled. Being-with-others is an essential constituent of man's being, i.e., as a possibility of being that is unavoidably present and taken up in every human activity. It would be impossible to retain either one's genuine humanity or one's sanity were one to act in such a way whereby, even implicitly, others were not taken into account. Every attitude we assume, every word we utter, and every act we undertake *establishes* us in relation to others. Our thoughts mold the image we have of ourselves in relation to others and our words and actions help suggest the impression that others have of us. But in these actual concrete relations with others we sometimes open the way to a fuller acceptance cf and greater concern for the other person, whereas sometimes we tend to retreat from him or her and close ourselves off to their plight. In *both* of these cases we exist in a mode of being-with-others, but in the first instance it is an authentic mode, whereas in the second it is inauthentic.

The root of all inauthentic manifestations of being-with-others is the attitude of self-concern.[11] It is in this state of mind that, either consciously or unconsciously, we reduce the central aim of all value and meaning to the accompiishment of the welfare of ourself alone. This attitude can operate very deviously even in the person who outwardly appears to be thoroughly altruistic. Despite all magnanimous commitments and generous deeds, it silently measures the ultimate worth of these things in terms of the personal satisfaction that results from them. It is the root of inauthentic being-with because it is primarily responsible in preventing our essential being-with-others from full and genuine expression. Self-concern is a distorted actualization of the possibility of being-with; for while actually with others it causes us to constantly turn away from them. Thus, in hindering the development of an essential human possibility, it thereby stunts and distorts the growth of the person as a whole.

A major feature of self-concern is that by introverting all attention upon the projects of oneself alone, it tends to reduce the presence of others to that of mere objects. The unique existence of the other is subordinated to a role that he or she plays as a figure in one's own personal drama. On occasion it seems that the numberless other people only exist on the exterior with sometimes the merest flicker of interiority, whereas I am thoroughly present as a unique interior being and my exterior is just an inadequate reflection of what I really am. Thus we have an I-It situation in which we no longer genuinely encounter another person, but another thing. Such is the underlying structure of inauthentic being-with-others which acts as the common foundation for the emotional and intellectual developments that subsequently emerge out of it. Basically a threefold fragmentation of self-concern is discernible, composed of desirous attachment, aversion, and indifference. In spite of their obvious differences, these three attitudes are all rooted in the underlying sense of the other as objectified, minimized, and subordinated to the far greater concern of I.

Desirous attachment sees the other as essentially desirable and seeks to draw him or her into one's possession or sphere of influence. Aversion, on the other hand, sees the other as essentially undesirable or even repulsive and attempts to remove the person from one's field of contact. Indifference is an attitude in which the other simply does not matter, and his suffering and joys are of absolutely no consequence. In this way our relationships with others are limited to the manipulation of a few individuals who impinge on the domain of our personal concern, and the ignoring of all the many others who fall outside of that domain.

One of the strongest and most dominant forms of desirous attachment is that of sexual desire, in which the other person is evaluated solely in his or her physical suitability for gratifying our sexual drive. However, all attempts, no matter how subtle, to induce others to submit to our will in order that we can then use them to further our own personal ambitions, are forms of desirous attachment. Aversion likewise ranges from deep-rooted hatred, to gentle persuasion aimed at removing another person who happens to be obstructing the path to the fulfillment of our desires. Indifference is neutral in the sense that it neither tries to attract nor to repel others, but it is nevertheless inauthentic because it does not *accept* others equally, as does equanimity, but *disregards* them equally. On the basis of desirous attachment, aversion, and indifference various other distorted and inauthentic attitudes towards others emerge: for example, avarice, jealousy, dishonesty, pretention, fear, cruelty, vengeance, and inconsideration.[12] Perhaps pride should also be mentioned here, not as an attitude derived from either desirous attachment, aversion, or indifference, but as another direct consequence of self-concern. It too establishes us in a fixed relation with regard to others, namely one of superiority. In pride we consciously elevate our own standing and concerns and look down upon others as essentially inferior.

With each of these examples we should bear in mind that they are not merely descriptions of the way certain psychological factors temporarily affect the personality and interpersonal relationships, but that they are attempts to reveal their character as inauthentic manifestations of a basic ontological structure. Aversion, for instance, is an existential posture grounded in the essential possibility of being-with-others. As such it determines the way we *are-in-the-world-with-others* at a particular moment. It does not produce merely a psychological disturbance restricted to the invisible boundaries of the mind. In the presence of aversion, self, world, and others 'shift perspective' with regard to each other. Everyday objects assume a harsh, menacing character, another person stands out from all the others and looms threateningly in our direction, we may feel suffocated and enclosed yet coiled to suddenly lunge out. In an inauthentic state of being-with, one's very being-in-the-world is torn and disrupted.

In actual fact it is hard, or at any rate unpleasant, to imagine an individual in whom no trace at all of positive and warm feelings remain, and whose relationships with others are totally inauthentic. Such a person would be referred to as 'inhuman.' In reality, we are composed of "an intricately entangled series of events that are tortuously dual." [13] However, we should not allow ourselves to be deceived by our outward show of 'civilized' manners and 'cultured' social behaviour into believing that self-concern, desirous attachment, aversion, and indifference are steadily losing their hold over us. It is important to recognize the extremely powerful and disruptive influence these elements have, and to realize that, to an extent far greater than we would like to admit, it is we who are dominated and controlled by *them*. Let us now see if it is possible to start disentangling this chaos of destructive tendencies and to discover a way to a more authentic being-with-others.

12. Authentic Being-With-Others

It is not possible to begin diminishing the influence of self-concern without first opening up an awareness of our being which experientially discloses the primal ground of relationship that lies far deeper than any trace of self-centeredness. It must be remembered that self-concern is an inauthentic distortion of the possibilities contained in that ground, and is thus a *subsequent* existential actualization of those essential possibilities. Hence an authentic being-with-others can only emerge out of an experiential encounter with an appeciation of that ground. Clearly this experience cannot be simply commanded at will. It is necessary to gradually spiral down to its depths. As a first step, the imbalance resulting from the three principal manifestations of self-concern—desirous attachment, aversion, and indifference—needs to be confronted and harmonized in equanimity.

Equanimity sees through the superficial veneer projected upon others by desirous attachment, aversion and indifference. Under the influence of these attitudes others actually appear to us as though desirability, repugnance, or insignificance were inherent characteristics of their vital essence. Desirability, for example, seems to pour forth from the very being of the desired person; it exudes from bodily movements, voice, laughter, hair, even from clothing. However, when one's desire has been satiated, it is distinctly unsettling how this supposedly essential quality can so swiftly evaporate and disappear, leaving one confronted with an insignificant or even a repugnant object-person. This jarring mutability of our inauthentic relationships is based upon the unrealistic imputation of subjectively tainted images upon others, and the subsequent confusion of what we have merely imagined for the sensuous reality of the other person's being. In this way we create a situation of unpredictably shifting imbalance in which some people are drawn close to us, others are thrust away, and the rest are members of an impersonal mass that do not have to be individually accounted for. The purpose of developing equanimity is to progressively break down this disproportionately structured state of interpersonal relations, and to replace it with one in which our grossest projections have been stripped away, where we find ourselves encountering the essentially equal being who had previously been concealed behind the masks we had shaped for them. Equanimity sees others as they are; no one is essentially desirable, no one is essentially repugnant, and no one is essentially insignificant. All are equally sentient beings, hoping and fearing, loving and hating, living and dying.

Equanimity can be gradually achieved through a systematic and concentrated analysis of the relations that we currently conduct with others. It is a question of bringing the person with whom we have a particular relationship—or in the case of indifference, a 'non–relationship'— to mind, then, having allowed the feeling that person evokes to arise, stepping back to a standpoint of detached objectivity. From this detached viewpoint one attempts to disentangle the actual person from the person as–he–appears–to–me–now. This is none too easy and requires repeated and sustained reflection on the situation from numerous different angles, trying to see the person from the vantage point of other people, or from the perspective of another time when we knew him differently. By extending this form of contemplation in ever widening circles so as to include all of those with whom we come into contact, a growing sense of equanimity will emerge in which the equalness of others slowly rises to the fore and their differences slip into the background.[14] However, equanimity should not be considered as an end in itself. Although it may peacefully reduce the tensions and conflicts inherent in desirous attachment and aversion, it hardly offers a richer interpersonal experience in return. It levels out certain unrealistic distinctions and accepts others equally, but in its detachment remains removed from any further active participation. As such it hovers at the threshold of authenticity in preparation for the next step: the task of constructing a meaningful pattern of relationship.

The balanced and accepting state of equanimity can be compared to a smooth clean wall that has been prepared as the surface for a painting through the careful removal of a previous image. The value of such a wall lies not in the uniform white expanse that covers it, but in its providing the possibility for the creation of a new image. Likewise equanimity should be seen as a mental state, realized through the cleansing of a disruptive pattern of relationship, which acts as the necessary foundation for the further construction of an authentic being–with–others. Once the adverse symptoms of desirous attachment, aversion, and indifference have been neutralized through equanimity, it is necessary to proceed even deeper and tackle the root of the problem, self–concern. The first stage in this process is to recognize the equality of self and other.

In equanimity we recognize the equality between others—between this person and that person; now this needs to be personalized in the recognition of the equality between oneself and others—between me and you. This involves realizing that just as I seek comfort, security and happiness, and wish to avoid suffering, fear and pain, so do you. Just as I feel worried, lonely, anxious, and shudder at the possibility of meaninglessness, so do you. It is a question of removing the massive load of importance that overweighs the scales in favour of myself and placing it piece by piece on the other pan of the balance. As with equanimity, this process requires repeated and sustained reflection on the situation from numerous different angles. Above all it requires a fundamental openness to the unique presence of living, feeling, conscious beings, an openness in which we start to perceive the other person as an end, rather than a means, a 'you' rather than an 'he' or a 'she.' And it is in the midst of such an openness that the following questions force themselves upon us: "When both myself and others are similar in that we

wish to be happy, what is so special about me? Why do
I strive for my happiness alone? And when both myself
and others are similar in that we do not wish to suffer,
what is so special about me? Why do I protect myself
and not others?" [15] However, such questions as these
do not arise as a result of intellectual speculation.
They are not posed with our thoughts and mouths
alone, but with our being.

What is being challenged here is the previously un-
questioned authority of self-concern. The provenance
of these questions is not a calculated series of deduc-
tive or inductive logical steps (although such proce-
dures may be partly instrumental in their emergence),
but a direct experience of a fundamental mode of our
being, namely, our being-with-others. It is only as a
conceptual reflection of this experiential realization of
our being-with that these questions erupt on the surface of our minds. Through the sustained contemplation of the equality of self and other we descend to a
depth at which we suddenly touch that essential reality: *we are with others.* This primal experience reveals
that the presence of others is not incidental but essential to our being. We do not just happen to 'bump
into' others, but are inescapably together with them in
the world. As this awareness dawns upon us, self-concern is seen to be a drifting alien body, untethered
from its moorings, that forms no part of who we really
are. It is dislodged from its position as the seemingly
indestructible center of motivation and turns out to
lack any ontological foundation. Instead of representing an essential element of our being, it in fact con-
ceals an essential element of our being.

The experiential awareness of this primal ground of
relationship, being-with-others, marks the turning
point from inauthentic to authentic being-with-others. The groundless and distorted nature of self-
concern (and by implication desirous attachment,

aversion, indifference, and all its other derivatives) is brought to light, and the possibility of ontologically grounded authentic relationship is opened up. Such an experience does not induce a response of mute passivity. It questions the way we are. Confronted with its uncompromising gaze we are forced into decision. Life, as the ongoing actualization of possibility, never stays at rest in the cradle of its essential structure, it reaches fulfillment only in 'ex-sistence'. Being-with–others is an essential structure, restricted to the dimension of possibility; but in the process of actualization it assumes an existential structure through which we actively participate in the world with others. The moment self-concern is disclosed as a distorted actualization of being-with that only obstructs the fulfillment of its potential, the unobstructed range of possibility contained in the ground of being-with is unveiled. As the full range of this possibility, no longer obstructed, naturally unfolds into an existential structure, the essentially passive *being-with*-others is inevitably transformed into an existentially active *being-for*-others. In the living field of concrete relations, this is then revealed as *concern* for others.[16] Moreover, just as the initial prearticulate encounter with being-with issued in a conscious questioning, likewise the initial prearticulate stirring of our being-with awakens to the full extent of its possibilities and may become conceptually manifest in such conclusions as, "Hence I should dispel the misery of others, because it is suffering, just like my own; and I should benefit others, because they are sentient beings, just like myself." [17]

In this way concern for others emerges as the root of authentic being-with, and counteracts the inauthentic distortion of self-concern. It does not arise solely as the result of certain conclusions logically derived from a set of ethical axioms, neither is it the rather insincere and forced response to a norm of behaviour imposed upon and expected from the individual members of a particular social or religious group. It is not motivated by the thought of any particular result and it seeks no acknowledgment of its deeds from others. Rather it is the undistorted actualization of a fundamental characteristic of our being and, as such, is quite spontaneous and natural. "Although acting for the sake of others," remarks Shāntideva, "neither astonishment nor conceit arise. It is like feeding oneself: there is no hope for anything in return." [18]

Nevertheless, self-concern does not just disappear as soon as the first spark of concern for others appears. However inauthentic it may be, it has buried its roots very deep within us and continuous perseverance is required to overcome it. The spontaneity of authentic concern for others is constantly threatened with obstruction and distortion by self-concern. The two concerns live within us side by side, contending with one another, and creating a tension which is felt in moments of anguished indecision when I am faced with the wordless choice of unconditionally moving out to you, or slyly recoiling into the shell of me. Thus a conscious effort has to be made to cultivate concern for others and reduce self-concern. This is achieved through the "exchange of self for other" in which one repeatedly puts oneself in the place of others and tries to see things from their perspective rather than one's own. According to Shāntideva, this involves contemplating the actual reversal of the roles of self and other, so that one comes to consider oneself as 'him' or 'her,' and others as 'I.' For example, having made this exchange, he reflects, "He is honoured, but I am not; I have not found wealth such as he. He is praised, but I am despised; he is happy, but I suffer." [19] In this way the plight of others is actually identified as our own, and selfish demands are clearly seen as an obstruction to the fulfillment of both our own and other's welfare. Concern for others is activated in response to the hardships, the suffering, and the pain of others. Its natural outflow increases in proportion to the diminishing of self-concern. Slowly, perhaps sporadically and unpredictably at first, it assumes the dimensions of loving kindness and compassion. Imperceptibly, as being-with-others is authentically actualized in concernful participation, the welfare of others comes to overshadow in importance the previously inalienable rights of self-interest.

The meaning of man's life, as we have seen, is not measured by what he *has*, but by what he *is*. No matter how many possessions we have amassed, how much wealth we have accrued, how respected and secure our position is in society, how numerous the pieces of information we have accumulated, in moments of lucidity we may still abruptly percieve the dreadful futility of it all, the overwhelming emptiness and pointlessness of such a life. Nor does well-being rest in the absorption in the world of particular entities and in the frenzied struggle to maintain the illusion that there we are safe, there no death can intrude, there is where everyone else is—and they cannot all be wrong. When our concern for others is really nothing more than a superficial attitude adopted for the sake of neutralizing our own moral scruples, inevitably will the welfare of others be indignantly proclaimed in terms of the same illusory standards upheld by ourselves. Just as I am happy because of what I possess, so must you be. Just as I am contentedly absorbed in a world of things, so must you be. The fulfillment of other's welfare is unquestioningly reduced to matters of material sufficiency, equal opportunity, and adequate education. For the poor, the oppressed, and the illiterate, such things are of obvious importance, *but never as ends in themselves.* As is becoming disturbingly evident in modern industrialized society, the increased presence of these things is no guarantee of a qualitatively fuller or more meaningful life. Their only real value lies in their providing a relatively stable basis upon which the inner aim of human life can be authentically pursued. But to subordinate what is human to that which is less than human—wealth, opportunity, knowledge—is thoroughly self-defeating; we end up destroying the very life we set out to save.

The genuine welfare of man, of both oneself and others, is found in the optimum actualization of the potentialities of his being. To exist in the fullest possible way in our aloneness as well as in our relations with others is the fulfillment of the inner aim of human life. This is the mode of being referred to as Buddhahood; a mode of being revealed through the awakening and life of Shākyamuni; the answer to the questions implied in our very existence; and the focal point of Buddhist hope and endeavor. In our aloneness we turn toward Buddhahood for refuge and adopt the Buddha, Dharma, and Sangha as principles around which to authentically redirect and restructure our lives. Now, as natural and deeply rooted concern searches for the means to genuinely fulfill the welfare of others, we are driven inevitably to the same point. Buddhahood, as the optimum mode of being, is the end point in which the two essential, interwoven strands of our being—being-alone and being-with—are purposefully fulfilled. It is the mode wherein both meaningful being-for-oneself and meaningful being-for-others are realized.[20] Through the process of actualizing Buddhahood we experience the inner authentication of our own existence as well as the ever increasing capacity to reveal this way to others in our words and deeds. It is in the acts of communicating to others the possibility, the means of actualizing, and the living presence of a fuller and more meaningful life, that one comes to actively participate in the realization of the welfare of others. Thus, by recognizing other's welfare to lie in the fulfillment of what they *are* rather than in what they could *have*, authentic concern for others aims at actualizing Buddhahood in order to be of the greatest benefit to others. This concern becomes the 'awakening mind,' i.e., the intention to realize Buddhahood for the sake of others, whereby being-with reaches its maximum possible level of authentication.

CHAPTER V

WISDOM AND METHOD

*Since wisdom without method and method
without wisdom have been termed 'bondage', one should never discard either of
them.*

Atīsha˙

13. The Unity of Being-Alone and Being-With

During the course of the previous two chapters a sense
of dualism may have emerged. Man, it may be
thought, is partitioned into two virtually independent
compartments, one which he experiences all alone, and
another which he shares with his fellow beings. It is
undeniable that a distinction exists between these two
dimensions, but we should not imagine that the pair of
conceptual boxes we have invented for the sake of this
explanation are precise duplicates of the concrete conditions of life that they attempt to describe. Life invariably bursts through the constructs of thought in
which we try to contain it, innocently eluding our
grasp in anomaly, paradox, ambiguity and contradiction. However precisely one may draw the line between the categories of being-alone and being-with in
one's thoughts, no such line is to be found neatly
etched into the sensuous being of man. In actual life
our diverse experiences are not classified into clearly
defined types, sets, or categories; they impinge upon,

merge into, and fluidly penetrate one another. At best our conceptual apparatus produces workable approximations that function well with their own limits. But once these approximations are raised to the position of absolutes and are imposed *upon* man, who is then expected to conform to *them*, they assume grotesque and demonic proportions. Life does not mechanically alternate between aloneness and participation, rather it embraces them both in an undivided unity. Being-alone and being-with are the delicate ontological strands which, when woven together, help form the complex fabric of life. Thus life is the unified whole of which they are the diverse parts and we, as living beings, always find ourselves in the paradoxical situation of being simultaneously *alone with others.*

In addition to being a unity of diverse ontological elements, life is continually actualizing the potential of these elements in time. As we have seen, this process of actualization may be either inauthentic or authentic. It becomes inauthentic when full ranges of possibility are overlooked in favor of the limited actualization of certain potentials, which allows us to avoid the full responsibility of our existence by restricting our concern to narrowly defined boundaries. In inauthentic being-alone we flee from facing the totality of our existence through absorption in the particular entities of the world; in inauthentic being-with we ignore our essential relatedness to others through indulging in self-concern. In both these cases the turning point from inauthenticity to authenticity is comprised of an experiential recognition and acceptance of the fundamental character of our being which we have been previously evading and distorting. We recognize and accept that we are inescapably alone in our birth and death and inescapably together in a world with others. It is only upon such a foundation that we are able to then proceed in authenticating our existence through grounding it in, and taking into account, the full range of our essential possibilities. In the dimension of our aloneness we anxiously turn our hope away from the things of the world and instead seek refuge in Buddha, Dharma and Sangha. In terms of our being-with we turn our concern away from the limited demands of self towards the fulfillment of the welfare of others through the actualization of Buddahood. Thus the taking of refuge becomes the basis for authentic being-alone, and an awakening mind the basis for authentic being-with.

The taking of refuge and the cultivation of an awakening mind are the very foundations of a complete Buddhist practice. By examining the underlying ontological structures in which they are rooted, we have established them to be firmly grounded in their essential constitution of man's being. Their fundamental character is also clearly indicated by what is probably the best-known and most frequently recited verse of prayer found throughout Tibetan Buddhism:

> I take refuge in Buddha, Dharma and
> the Supreme Community
> Until the attainment of Enlightenment;
> Through the virtue of my deeds such
> as giving
> May I realize Buddhahood for the sake
> of the world.[2]

This verse—or one very similar—is invariably intoned as a preparation for personal prayer and contemplation as well as before engaging in any collective worship, ceremony, or ritual. It serves to remind the devotee of the basic motivation and commitment that are the prerequisites for any further spiritual development. And if the words are genuinely taken to heart, they should not invoke merely a superficial change in attitude, but a renewed sense of our existential reorientation. A further indication of the unique role of the taking of refuge and the cultivation of an awakening mind as the structural foundations for authentic being-alone and being-with, respectively, is that—apart from disciplines of a purely ethical character—they are the only stages of practice for which there exist formal ceremonies of acceptance. On these occasions the radical change in direction of one's existence is explicitly confirmed in the presence of the community, the Sangha. It is thereby established with full consciousness in one's own mind and at the same time provided with the supportive and protective conditions of the community whereby it is enabled to develop with minimum obstruction. The taking of refuge and the cultivation of an awakening mind are thus regarded as the two gateways to Buddhist practice; the former being the entrance to Buddhist life in general, and the latter being the entrance to the Bodhisattva path in particular.

In this way the concepts 'being-alone' and 'being-with' create a framework within which the basic constructs of the Buddhist path are seen to be grounded in the ontological structure of man and to cover the entire range of human potential. But again, it should not be supposed that taking refuge is exclusively restricted to a sealed compartment of aloneness, and an awakening mind to an equally self-enclosed region of participation. The notions of 'being-alone' and 'being-with-others' attempt to describe the essential structures of possibility that determine the way we actually are. But, although a concrete existential attitude may be founded in one or the other of these essential regions, in lived experience it invariably embraces both. Thus, taking refuge is primarily centered around authentically resolving a conflict confronted in the solitude of our aloneness, while at the same time it inevitably affects our participation in the world with others. By the very act of taking refuge, we enter into a community of faith, thereby identifying with and joining others who are likewise committed. Also, as part of this commitment, a particular ethical disposition is encouraged which thereby directly affects attitude towards, and relations with, others. Likewise, although the cultivation of an awakening mind is principally an authentic response to our essential being-with-others, it is nevertheless composed of an inner determination, resolve, and sense of orientation that are experienced solely by oneself.

Once present together, the taking of refuge and the cultivation of an awakening mind necessarily interpenetrate and complement one another. As soon as concern for others becomes an awakening mind, the motivation for taking refuge ceases to be restricted to the hope to resolve only our individual anxiety. Having experienced the equality of self and other, we hope to resolve the anxiety that is equally felt by others. This hope is fulfilled by aiming our life towards Buddhahood, and accomplishing this goal through the practice of Dharma in the supportive environment provided by the Sangha. Thus, although the dynamic structure of taking refuge remains unaltered, an awakening mind infuses that structure with a wholeness by causing it to embrace the total range of human potential Similarly, the structure of taking refuge provides concern for others with the framework within which to reach its optimum expression in an awakening mind. The recognition of Buddhahood as the optimum mode of being both for oneself and for others, which is implied within the act of taking refuge, is a necessary precondition for the development of an awakening mind. Hence the aspiration to realize Buddhahood for the sake of others can only arise within the preexistent context of having taken refuge. In this way a unity is revealed between taking refuge and an awakening mind that serves to dispel any sense of dualism.

Life is the ongoing actualization of potential being. When this actualization is limited and distorted, evading the responsibility of recognizing and accepting the full range of human potential, it is regarded as inauthentic. Conversely, an authentic process of actualization is one that faces up to the entire scope of our possibilities and aims at their optimum fulfillment in Buddhahood. To realize this aim, the process of authentic actualization needs to develop all elements of human potential and effectively counteract any obstructive tendencies towards continued inauthentic existence. Throughout the duration of this process a tension inevitably occurs between the incompatible directions pursued by these two movements. As long as potential remains undeveloped or obstructed, the optimum state of being will remain unrealizable. In the case of being-alone, as long as there is any evasive tendency towards seeking security in particular entities, meaningful being–for–oneself will be impossible. In the case of being-with, even the subtlest form of self-concern will preclude the fullest realization of meaningful being–for–others.

This last point is of particular significance. The presence of self-concern, however slight, prevents the authentic actualization of being–with and thereby the realization of the optimum mode of being, Buddhahood. Moreover, in order to bring the full range of our being–with–others to fulfillment, it is insufficient to merely neutralize self-concern; it has to be positively transformed into concern for others. For as long as concern for others is less than total, the presence of self-concern will still be detected. Therefore, fully authentic being–with requires *total and unconditional* concern for others, or, as stated in the traditional formula, that one aspires to attain Buddahood for the sake of *all sentient beings without exception*. This ontological interpretation serves to clarify the Mahāyāna doctrine of 'one final vehicle'.[3] The proponents of this view maintain that all spiritual paths must ultimately culminate in the way of the Bodhisattva. Even the Arhats, resting in the peace of nirvāna, will be aroused from their blissful absorption and urged to continue further to the final goal of Buddhahood. This is clearly stated in the *Saddharmapundarīkasūtra* where the Buddha is quoted as announcing that "Shrāvakas do not pass into nirvāna. They will all become Buddhas after having practiced the Bodhisattva life."[4] In the light of our consideration of being-with-others as an essential constituent of man's being, and of Buddhahood as the optimum actualization of potential being, this point of view—which outwardly may appear to be a mere dogmatic statement of the superiority of a particular school—is seen to have a firm ontological foundation. In fact, it now becomes clear why a discipline that stops short of anything less than total concern for others could be called a 'lesser vehicle' (*Hīnayāna*), and why ultimately such a concern must inevitably be adopted.

As the primal crystallizations of authentic being-alone and being-with, the taking of refuge and the cultivation of an awakening mind are the foundations upon which the process of all further actualization of potential is supported. To be complete and effective, this process, referred to as the 'path', must correlate with the structure of its foundations. Thus it is described in terms of 'wisdom' (*prajñā*) and 'method' (*upāya*), the former denoting the development of authentic being-alone, and the latter the development of authentic being-with. As with the taking of refuge and the cultivation of an awakening mind, wisdom and method are neither exclusively restricted to the domains of being-alone and being-with, respectively, nor should they be considered as operating independently of one another. They mutually assist the growth of each other: wisdom endows method with intelligence and discrimination, method supplies the secure foundation upon which wisdom is able to discern its object with calm and penetration. Their relationship is compared to that of a cripple with good eyesight (wisdom) being carried on the shoulders of a physically fit blindman (method). The cripple can see clearly but has no means of conveyance, and the fit man can walk without difficulty but is unable to see where he is going. It is only by working together that either of them can manage to go anywhere. Likewise, the process of authentication of potential can only effectively reach its goal through the mutual cooperation of its two principal aspects, wisdom and method.

14. Wisdom

Wisdom and method can be explained by means of their division into the six transcending functions (*paramitā*). Two of these, the transcending functions of concentration and wisdom, constitute 'wisdom'; and the remaining four, giving, moral discipline, patience, and enthusiasm, make up the practice of 'method'.[5] Since the components of wisdom are grounded in the solitude of the mind, consideration of them leads us into the domain of psychology; whereas an analysis of the aspects of method, which are founded in our being–with–others, lead us into the realm of ethics.

"Mind is chief," declares the first line of the *Dhammapada*, "it is the precursor of all conditions both good and evil."[6] From the outset the teachings of Buddhism have constantly emphasized the preeminence of psychological factors in determining the way we are. Distorted, unrealistic psychological attitudes are at the root of our inauthentic modes of being, whereas systematic purification and transformation of such attitudes constitutes the inner momentum of the path that culminates in the optimum state of being. More specifically, it is the discerning insight of wisdom united with the single-pointed absorption of concentration that forms the essential driving force of this momentum. However, to fully grasp their significance in this process it is necessary to appreciate the psychological context in which they operate.

The mind operates in a twofold manner. It perceives and it conceives. Here 'perception' refers to the basically receptive, prereflective dimension of mind in which the world, its objects, and other people appear to be presented to us. 'Conception' denotes the responsive and reflective capacity of mind through which we react to our encounter with the world.[7] This means that, on the one hand, we see colors and shapes, hear sounds, experience tactile sensations, and so forth and, on the other hand, we think about them, judge them, and respond to them emotionally. Actual lived experience does, of course, not admit of such a straightforward duplicity. In practice these processes are inextricably interwoven. Moreover, they mutually determine each other's content and character. Our conceptions of the world affect our perceptions of the world which, in turn, condition the way we subsequently conceive the world. However, it is certain conceptions that are initially responsible for the inauthenticity, disruption and conflict within our existence. Thus the process of conceptualization needs to be clarified before any attempt can be made to untangle the knots of psychological distortion in which it has caught us.

The range of the term 'conception' is here extended to cover *all* psychological responses that we make to what is presented to consciousness. Its meaning is not restricted merely to superficial intellectual functions but encompasses conscious thoughts as well as the less articulate emotional responses such as desire, anger, pride and so forth. Conception is distinguished from bare perception by the presence of subjectively toned 'ideas' or 'images' [8] that appear to be merged inseparably with whatever we happen to be conscious of. In thinking about the world we organize it in accordance with our preconceptions, we evaluate and categorize it so that it appears to correspond to the way we are habitually used to viewing it. Our emotional relation to the content of our experience does not interpret and classify but rather colours the world in shades of meaning that are only subsequently expressed in words. Thoughts and ideas enable us to construct and have access to multifaceted 'dimensions' that transcend the spatial and temporal limitations of particular concrete situations. Although physically restricted to this small room partially illuminated by a desk lamp, I *live* in a geographical location, in a society with legal and political structures, in the framework of a history, and in the context of religious and philosophical beliefs. But in addition to allowing us this freedom from our environmental limits, conception is also responsible for deeply rooted distortions that keep us in a state of bondage to an unbroken cycle of anxiety, frustration, and suffering. No matter how complex, extensive, and rarified the various conceptual dimensions we inhabit become, as long as these fundamental distortions of conception are not rectified we will be unable to escape from the intrusions of an underlying sense of uneasiness and despair.

A conceptual distortion is characterized by the fact that the idea through which it conceives of its object is not an accurate representation of that object. Since this idea seems to be inseparably merged with the nature of the object, we are then unable to distinguish the object from our mistakenly conceived idea of the object. Now, even as we perceive the object with our senses, it appears to us in a certain way that in fact has been fabricated by our own conceptualization. But we unquestioningly assent to the veracity of our sense experiences and proceed to build up a structured relationship with the world of our experience that in fact is founded upon erroneous assumptions. Such a situation inevitably gives rise to confusion, conflict, and frustration. We perceive the world in a particular way and confidently expect it to conform to its appearance. But we fail to recognize that certain aspects of the 'reality' that appear to us are nothing but figments of our own imagination. In this confusion a conflict ensues between the world as it is and the world as we believe it to be. And the more we insist on our infallibility, the more frustrated we become as the actual world again and again stubbornly refuses to live up to our expectations. Once we assent to a distorted conception of ourselves, the world, or others, we immediately create a disharmonious situation in which two totally incompatible worlds are unquestioningly assumed to be identical. The greater the rift becomes between the world as it is and the world as we imagine and want it to be, the more heightened becomes our sense of basic insecurity, alienation and anxiety. Thus psychological disturbance increases in direct proportion to conceptual distortion.

Suppose that I have a very dishonest and malevolent neighbor who is only intent upon my harm. However, he wins my confidence and friendship through an appearance of being kind and helpful. As long as I assume that his outward appearance is an honest representation of his inner motives, I will be constantly deceived, confused, and hurt by his actions since they contradict the image I have of him. Only when I cease to insist on his genuineness and come to understand his real intentions, will I no longer be fooled by appearances and will I be able to effectively deal with the situation.[9] This is a fairly common problem that most of us are subjected to once in a while, and one that we can often resolve and soon forget about. However, it serves to illustrate a similar mode of conception that exists at a much deeper instinctive level, namely *ignorance*. As such, ignorance is not merely a deficiency of knowledge but, in addition, it positively apprehends reality in a distinctive way. And being a distorted mode of conception, it creates a view of the world what is in opposition to, and in conflict with, the actual way the world is. Deeply enmeshed within the mind, it permeates every thought, emotion, and perception, producing an instinctive sense of oneself and the world which is so familiar that it is never noticed.

Ignorance is often regarded as being constituted of three principal aspects. These are: the apprehension of what is impermanent to be permanent; the apprehension of what is unsatisfactory to be satisfactory; and the apprehension of what is without a self-identity to have a self-identity.[10] The first of these, the notion of permanence, refers to our instinctive sense of a non-momentary, static, unchanging, and fixed-in-time character that seems to inhere within ourselves and in the world. Although we intellectually 'know' that both our person and the objects of the world are transient and doomed to destruction, we habitually *behave* as though the contrary were true. During the unreflecting course of daily life, our thoughts, our plans, our conversations, and our actions all reflect the self-assured confidence of an immortal for whom death is eternally absent. Confronted with a world composed of seemingly durable, essentially unchanging elements, we sense that real satisfaction must lie in manipulating these elements in such a way that we construct the 'perfect' situation. The situations we habitually find ourselves in are always to some extent unsatisfactory, yet it seems to us that merely certain modifications would solve the problems that happen to disturb or irritate us. But however much we reorganize this and change that, eliminate one thing and introduce another, the perfect final arrangement forever eludes us. An unexpected event suddenly interrupts, a previously unnoticed incompatibility starts to glare uncomfortably, we discover that we cannot rely upon such a person after all. Or if the external situation seems at last to be in order, a vague aching sense of boredom and uneasiness may fleetingly taunt us in the pit of the stomach. We may feel suddenly imprisoned and lonely among the frozen images of our own design. Whatever the case, we rarely pay any heed to these inconsistencies, but swiftly cover them up with the habitual screens of our mental and verbal chatter. We continue to insist that the final solution is just around the next corner, waiting for us in the arms of the salesman or perhaps the psychiatrist. In this way we mistakenly apprehend the manipulation of particular entities to be essentially capable of producing satisfaction, when in fact it is not so. Underlying both of the above misconceptions—those of permanence and satisfactoriness—is the sense of a peculiar self-identity residing in the very core of things. This basic form of ignorance causes oneself, others and the objects of the world to appear as though they were entirely self-sufficient and independent of all conditioning factors, component elements, and conceptual organization. This is the fundamental misconception upon which the entire edifice of samsāra rests.

When we try and imagine the instinctive 'natural' world that quietly yet massively abides in the background of all our sophisticated thinking, we see that, despite all enlightened speculation about 'I', *I* remain untouched. I feel as though I subsist independently of my body and my mind as an indeterminate yet concrete something consisting of countless involuting layers of itself. From the way you look at me, from the way you act, I suppose that it is more or less the same for you. Likewise, all inanimate objects seem to exude an identity from somewhere deep within themselves that sufficiently defines their essence without having to refer to anything else. The world is thus inhabited by numberless self-enclosed entities that with no apparent meaning always find themselves together. Such an apparent self-sufficiency is readily translated into a static and abiding permanence. In addition, having recognized those things that cause harm as 'inherently undesirable' and those that give pleasure as 'inherently desirable', it appears that suffering could be eliminated and lasting satisfaction gained through the simple process of rejection and acceptance. Consequently, we fill our lives with plans and projects to manipulate the self-contained chunks of the world to our best advantage. Motivated by desirous attachment for what we want, and aversion towards what we dislike, we absorb ourselves in the task of building up the 'perfect' situation around the cherished unchanging kernel of the self. As long as we continue to believe in the possibility of success, our interest and enthusiasm remain, shielding us from the threat of anxiety or doubts. But should a gap suddenly open up and disclose to us the essential futility of such an approach to life, the bleak landscape of ignorance will stand before us: the world of numberless unrelated self-enclosed things.

Stripped for the moment of the intricate covering of our memories, plans, disguises and justifications, we experience anxiety in the face of a world devoid of promise, empty of any sense, cold, and uninviting. Here we feel the loneliness of our inherent separation from others, and the alienation from what is closest to us, our very bodies and minds. Habitually, such feelings are hurriedly dismissed and covered up again as soon as they even dimly begin to stir. But if they are allowed to enter the articulate domain of consciousness and unveil what they behold, we are presented with the sheer senseless abundance of objects that may, in the words of Sartre, strike us as 'nauseating', 'absurd', and 'superfluous.' [11] Some existentialist writers conclude that what appears in these moments of anxiety is the true nature of reality, and then go on to posit authentic existence as an heroic resignation to this fact in which one continues to live despite the basic absurdity and meaninglessness of everything one does. However, although they may no longer cling to the illusion that permanence and satisfaction inhere in such a world, they still assent to the validity of its basic appearance as being composed of unrelated self-existent entities. Their attitude to existence, however depressive it may be, is at least logically consistent with the view that oneself, others, and the objects of the world have such an independent self-identity.

Our initial authentic response to anxiety is to direct our hope away from the particular entities of the world towards the refuge of Buddha, Dharma, and Sangha. Subsequently, through following the path of Dharma, one will be led back to the task of confronting and resolving this anxiety at its very roots. *Anxiety is the mood of ignorance.*[12] This is evident from the three aspects of anxiety we have considered so far. The instinctive anxiety that drives us into concernful absorption with the world of particular things is the mood of the instinctive ignorance that, in the face of existence in its totality, evades the full range of ontological possibility by fabricating a world of self-existent entities, thereby acting as the basis for flight into samsāra. The intensified anxiety, which erupts when one glimpses the total extent of one's existence—one's birth and death—and realizes that the absorption into the world of things is vain, is the mood experienced in those moments when the incompatibility between the world fabricated by ignorance and the actuality of one's birth and death is felt. Finally, when ignorance directly stares out into the bleak world of self-existent, unrelated entities, the mood that overcomes us is that of anxiety. Therefore, it is only through counteracting ignorance that anxiety can be dispelled. And this is the very function and aim of wisdom.

The origin of the conflict, frustration, and anxiety we experience does not lie in the nature of the world itself but in our distorted conceptions of the world. In assenting to the way the world instinctively appears, we naturally assume that the cause of suffering and meaninglessness inhere within it, whereas it is the very act of assenting that is actually to blame. It is an ironic situation in which we sincerely believe the enemy to be surrounding our house, when in fact he is sitting comfortably indoors. To authentically solve the problem it is necessary to turn our attention away from the task of struggling with a stubborn and intractable world and to turn it instead to dispelling the ignorance that mistakenly causes such a world to appear. Wisdom is the gaining of understanding and insight that progressively pierce through the veil of ignorance. It brings our view of the world into accordance with the world as it is and thereby removes the conflict and frustration attendant upon ignorance. Wisdom concentrates primarily on clearly discerning the characteristics of impermanence, unsatisfactoriness and self-identitylessness. Lasting and stable peace of mind is achieved not through discovering the permanence of anything, but through fully accepting the impermanent *as* impermanent and ceasing to insist that it is otherwise. Likewise, genuine contentment is found in realizing that what one previously assumed to be capable of providing satisfaction is actually unable to do so. It is in accepting this fact and not in an ever more strenuous attempt to force the world into an impossible shape that a realistic outlook is achieved which ceases to expect from the world something the world can never provide. Paradoxically, in this very act of acceptance one finds the happiness that had always eluded one before. But it is insight into the lack of self-identity that finally undermines the instinctive misconceptions we have of ourselves, others, and the world. Through revealing that nothing at all is characterized by an independent, self-sufficient identity, the desolate image of numerous isolated, unrelated entities is dispelled. As this new vision unfolds, our basic anxiety and our sense of meaninglessness are dissolved in the growing awareness of the profound mystery of interrelatedness that permeates all phenomena.

The understanding of the lack of any self-sufficient inherent identity within things is referred to as the understanding of 'voidness' (shūnyatā). The term 'voidness' denotes the simple lack of the falsely imagined self-identity. To cognize voidness means to realize that the self-identity of things, which instinctively seemed so real, is actually non-existent. Moreover, this voidness (of a self-identity existing independently of causes, component parts, and conceptual organization) implicitly reveals the universal character of dependency upon such things. Therefore, 'voidness' describes, in a negative way, the fundamental characteristic of all phenomena that allows them to be. In a positive way the nature of this be-ing is most clearly intimated by the notion of 'dependent arising'. Therefore, voidness is not the equivalent to nothingness, or non-being, but in the actual way phenomena *are*, namely, void of a falsely fabricated self-identity. Neither is it a transcendent absolute or a pre-existent ground of being that underlies the manifestation of all particular entities. Rather it is a characteristic immanent in all phenomena that is obscured from us by the distorting influence of ignorance and brought to light by wisdom. As soon as a phenomenon ceases to be, its voidness of self-identity ceases to be. Thus there is no voidness subsisting in a realm of its own apart from the empirical world.

The aim of wisdom is to gain freedom from the bondage of ignorance by clearly discerning the suchness of ourselves and the world, concealed by the distortions of ignorance. Since it is a question of understanding the unreality of a fallacious mode of appearance, the initial step is to recognize exactly how this false appearance—that of an inherent self-identity—appears. Only when this has been clearly identified, can we proceed, by means of conceptual analysis and heightened perceptual awareness, to ascertain its utter absence and voidness. Without first identifying precisely what is to be negated there is the danger of succumbing to either a nihilist position of denying the validity and meaning of everything, or an incomplete rejection in which we only partially solve the problem. At the outset it is recommended that this analysis and awareness are applied to oneself, because the instinctive conception of our own inherent self-identity is the most dominant and thus the most disruptive form of ignorance. However, this apprehension of our self-identity, which is often called 'self-grasping',[13] should not be confused with self-concern. Self-grasping is a misconception that needs to be brought to a complete stop through perceiving the non-existence of its object, whereas self-concern needs to be *transformed* into concern for others.

Our distorted conceptions of permanence, satisfactoriness, and self-identity are very deeply rooted and create an instinctive 'sense' of how we and the world are that is impervious to merely a superficial change of view. No matter how intellectually convinced we are of a belief superstructure that incorporates tenets such as, 'All phenomena lack self-identity', this certainty alone is unable to effect a lasting transformation in the way we are. Neither sustained intellectual reflection upon nor occasional perceptual glimpses into voidness are able to affect the instinctive sense of an abiding self-identity that constantly envelops us. In order for such insights to be fully integrated, they need to be unified with one-pointed concentration (samādhi). In this way they are enabled to penetrate to the emotional and instinctive levels of our being and thereby affect not only our intellectual attitudes but our deepest sense of how and what we are. Although initially the cultivation of concentration may take place independently of the development of wisdom, it is only of any real value when it comes to be unified with wisdom, thereby providing it with the power of stability and penetration. By itself the progressive achievement of the various stages of concentration can lead to different states of absorption that offer a degree of inner calm and tranquillity. But without the incisive quality of wisdom these states are unable to rectify the instinctive misconceptions that bind us to the disruptive and painful condition of samsāra. A passage from Tzong Khapa clearly states this point:

> One-pointed absorption alone does not have the ability to sever the roots of samsāra. Yet however much analysis is carried out by wisdom which is separated from the path of calm concentration, the disturbing conceptions will not be dispelled. Therefore, one should mount the wisdom which clearly discerns the way things are upon the immovable horse of calm concentration.[14]

15. Method

Although wisdom and concentration are cultivated in the region of one's aloneness, their effective development requires a sound ethical basis which is founded in one's relations with others. In order for wisdom to be deeply penetrating it needs the support of a concentrated mind that is not distracted by uncontrolled thoughts and emotions. Calm concentration, in turn, can only be realized within the framework of an ethical discipline that maintains one's conduct within certain boundaries. Unrestrained behaviour only serves to further aggravate the disturbances and tensions in the mind, thus making the cultivation of calm concentration all the more difficult. Thus one important function of ethics in Buddhism is that of outlining a mode of conduct conducive to the development of concentration and the heightening of wisdom. In this way an ethical conduct acts as a necessary prerequisite for the achievement of the inner aim of the path.

The ethical practices of 'method' are founded in the ontological structure of being-with, and as such must pertain to the actualization of authentic being-with-others. This is partially achieved through their acting as a supportive condition for the wisdom that forms the essential momentum of the process of realizing Buddhahood. For the aim of an awakening mind—meaningful being for others—is only fulfilled in the actualization of Buddhahood. But in addition, active participation in the lives of others is demanded in order to incorporate the full range of human potential into spiritual life. Penetrating insight into voidness may be the essential factor in the awakening to meaningful being for oneself, but if it lacks a comparably evolved framework in which to express itself in words and deeds, it falls short of the goal of optimal human being. The aim of the method aspect of practice is to systematically construct such a framework in conjunction with the cultivation of wisdom and concentration. This involves a wide number of activities, ranging from the formation of coherent patterns of thought, which then enable lucid vocal communication to take place, to the ability to selflessly give one's physical assistance to others in need. The unified practice of wisdom and method can thus be understood as the simultaneous authentication of the potentials of one's being-alone and being-with. In fact the simultaneous and complementary development of wisdom and method is essential to the growth of a fully integrated practice. Returning tc Atīsha's statement, to cultivate one, independently of the other, is to remain in bondage. Wisdom that neglects method leads to excessive introversion and an inability to effectively communicate with others. Method without wisdom can produce well-intentioned but naive and superficial acts of altruism that alleviate merely the symptoms of suffering without tackling the root cause of the problem.

The practices relating to method are covered by the remaining four of the six transcendent functions: giving, moral discipline, patience, and enthusiasm.

Giving is the intention to turn away from one's own self-interest and to freely and willingly give what one has to others. Essentially it involves a transformation of attitude. Instead of a centripetal longing that constantly seeks to draw everything inward towards oneself at the center, giving is a centrifugal longing that seeks to expel everything away from oneself into the hands of others. It needs to become a basic orientation of our life, thereby embracing not merely overt acts of generosity, but the giving of words of advice, the giving of care and protection, the giving of kindness and love. Furthermore, it is not restricted to concrete interpersonal situations but can be developed in private contemplation and prayer. The principal function of such exercises is to firmly establish an inner sense of altruistic resolve by means of consciously directing one's attention away from oneself to others and sincerely wishing for their well-being instead of one's own. This culminates in the intention of an awakening mind to actualize Buddhahood for the sake of others. Thereby, both body and mind are dedicated to the welfare of others. The great danger here, though, is that such altruism, generated in the seclusion of one's own thoughts, becomes a subtle means of evading concrete inter-personal responsibility and of justifying to oneself a life of peaceful uninvolved isolation from others. We proclaim to ourselves our love and compassion for such abstract entities as 'humanity' or 'all sentient beings' in order to avoid having to love any one person. It is important, therefore, that first and foremost giving be practised in the concrete sphere of life among the people one encounters from day to day. It should not be allowed to evaporate into the rarified atmosphere of idealism.

Moral discipline is a compound of two principal functions, those of restraint and activity. Restraint involves the maintaining of one's conduct within certain prescribed boundaries. These boundaries are fixed according to the disposition of the individual. In each case they should provide a defined space of action in which that person is enabled to most effectively actualize the process of the path. The various boundaries correspond to the various sets of vows or moral precepts: those of the laity, the novice, the monk, the nun, the Bodhisattva, the yogin, and so forth. The essence of moral discipline is not merely the control of one's outward behavior but the control of the psychological factors that are responsible for the overt acts of body and speech. To achieve such control requires the development of constant mindfulness of the moral boundary one has accepted for oneself and ever present alertness to watch for any disruptive mental factors that may cause one to transgress that boundary.[15] With the presence of such mindfulness and alertness the grosser disturbances of the mind can be avoided, thus creating a basic tranquillity in which concentration and wisdom can be effectively cultivated. The second aspect of moral discipline is that of activity. This is the positive counterpart to restraint that is enabled to operate because of the calm borders established through restraint while at the same time adding further strength to those boundaries. Generally speaking, this activity refers to any actualization of authentic being that forms part of the path. More specifically, it involves the cultivation of the positive counterparts to whatever one is attempting to restrain from. If one's restraint includes refraining from taking life, for example, the positive counterpart would be to consciously save and protect life. In this way the task of restraint is obviously facilitated and strengthened.

Patience is the specific antidote to anger and hatred. It is an attitude of accepting both the harm caused by others and the pains and discomforts found in life instead of angrily retaliating against them. Only in the calm afforded by patient acceptance is one able to clearly discern the nature of the situation and proceed to deal with it realistically. Once the mind becomes distorted and disturbed with anger, any possibility of objectivity is lost. One consequently embarks upon a course of action grounded in misconception that inevitably leads to a heightening of the initial conflict rather than its resolution. Patience is not an indifferent quietism that passively accepts all harm. It should be seen as the necessary precondition for any constructive response to the difficulties and problems we encounter in our relations with others and the world. To a large extent patient acceptance is based upon the recognition that no lasting solution can be found through an obstinate manipulation of the entities of the world alone. Without any reconsideration of the validity of our own assumptions concerning the nature of those entities, no such solution will ever be forthcoming.[16]

Enthusiasm is defined as joy in the pursuit of what is wholesome. It is the energy that propels and sustains the process of actualizing the path. But this is not tight-lipped perseverance or strenuous effort which forces one into a rigidly fixed discipline that one instinctively rejects. It should be the spontaneous response that naturally emerges once certain insights into the structure of being have been gained. The awareness of the inevitability of death confronts us with our open yet limited possibilities. In the acceptance of Buddha as the optimum actualization of these possibilities and of Dharma as the means of authentically actualizing them, we adopt an existential commitment. The fulfillment of this commitment then depends upon two things: the *aspiration* to realize the possibilities that lie ahead, and the *self-confidence* that acknowledges one's freedom and ability to realize them, thus dispelling the sense of being immutably imprisoned in the structure of one's facticity. Such aspiration gives a meaningful direction to one's life, and self-confidence provides the conviction that one is actually capable of *making* one's life meaningful. In this context a joyous dedication to the task in hand arises, which Shāntideva compares to that of a child in play, or of an elephant tormented by the sun plunging into a cool lake. [17] It is these three factors of aspiration, self-confidence, and joy, together with the ability to recognize when one has reached one's limits and needs to rest, that constitute the essence of enthusiasm.[18]

Through consideration of the six transcending functions we are not merely presented with six isolated factors that need to be cultivated in order for us to actualize Buddhahood. Rather there emerges an integral psychological portrait of the Bodhisattva, the individual who seeks the optimum state of being for the sake of others. The six transcending functions stand as six principal structural features of his character which are interwoven with the other elements of his personality. The Bodhisattva should be characterized by an open, outgoing generosity, tempered by mindfulness and ethical restraint. He should be accepting and submissive, yet fired by a natural, joyous enthusiasm. His mind should be discerning and critical, yet rooted in a deep inner calm. This is the model upon which we strive to pattern our lives as we engage in the actualization of the path. But this model is subordinate to an even superior model; the optimum mode of being towards which the Boddhisattva's way of life itself is aimed.

CHAPTER VI

THE OPTIMUM MODE OF BEING

A monk asked the Zen Master Shan, "Who is the Buddha?" "He is an old monk of the Western country." "What is enlightenment?" Shan gave the questioner a blow saying, "You get out of here; do not scatter dirt around us!"[1]

16. The Two Bodies of the Buddha

The phrase 'the optimum mode of being' is a way of decontaminating the misused and misunderstood term 'Buddha'. As we have seen, 'Buddha' or 'Buddhahood' refers to a mode of being in which all that is disruptive and distorted has been eliminated, and all that is to be actualized has been actualized. This is clear from the etymology of the Tibetan term of 'Buddha', *sangs. rgyas.*, which means 'purified-fulfilled'. The state of Buddhahood is one in which inauthentic modes of being have been purified and the potentials for authentic modes of being have been fulfilled. In accordance with the twofold division of being–alone and being–with, this optimum state of being is compounded of optimum being–alone and optimum being–with–others. Optimum being-alone is referred to by the expression 'the actualization of meaningful being for oneself' or 'the dharma–body' (*dharmakāya*). Whereas optimum being–with–others is expressed by the terms 'the actualization of meaningful being for others' or 'the form-body' (*rūpakāya*). The inseparable and essentially interwoven character of the dharma-body and the form-body is indicated by the fact that they are always realized simultaneously and never independently.

Buddhahood is thus comprised of two principal modes of being, called the 'dharma-body' and the 'form-body', that correspond to the states of optimum being-alone and optimum being-with respectively. The 'dharma-body' refers to the inner, private insight into the nature of oneself, others, and the world, experienced in the optimum mode of being. Its private character, and thereby its location in the dimension of aloneness, is illustrated by the traditional dogma which states that the dharma-body is only accessible to the Buddhas themselves.[2] It is a state of consciousness in which the distortions of ignorance have been dispelled by means of the transcending function of wisdom. One is thus constantly grounded in an awareness of the voidness of any self-sufficient existence inhering within the core of things. By implication one is also deeply conscious of the dependent and relative nature of whatever is experienced. It is in this context that the meaning of the 'omniscience' of Buddha is to be understood. This is clear from the *Pitāputrasamā-gamasūtra*, which states,

"The Tathāgata understands both the conventional and ultimate truths. . . . However, the Lord is said to be 'omniscient' because he fully sees, fully knows, and has well realized (the ultimate truth), voidness."[3]

Being an optimum mode of consciousness, it is evident that the dharma-body is primarily the result of wisdom, as opposed to method. As such it is the peak experience, the goal and the focal-point towards which wisdom, in union with concentration, is constantly aiming. Through the realization of the dharma-body the hope that constitutes the essential dynamic of taking refuge is fulfilled, and thereby meaningful being-for-oneself is achieved. This comes about through the resolution of the conflict between the world as it is and the world as it is imagined to be in ignorance. Once ignorance has been purified through wisdom, the mood of anxiety that was felt in the deepest recesses of this conflict is dissolved. Thus the dharma-body is grounded in the immediate 'mystical' experience of oneself and the world *as they are.* And instead of anxiety, joy becomes the underlying mood of one's being-in-the-world. In this way the dharma-body stands as the culminating point of the process of actualizing authentic being-alone. The anxiety, which was the cause for taking-refuge, is overcome through the wisdom that dispels ignorance and, thereby, the hope of finding meaningful being-for-oneself is fulfilled.

The 'form-body' refers to the mode of being-with-others that is manifest in the optimum mode of being, Buddhahood. Just as the dharma-body is the aspect of Buddhahood restricted to one's own experience, the form-body is the aspect of Buddhahood accessible to the experience of others. As the actualization of meaningful being-for-others, the form-body encompasses all the ways in which a person who has realized the optimum mode of being appears to those with whom he is actively involved. Generally speaking, such a person is characterized by three principal qualities. He appears to be possessed of great intuition and wisdom, he radiates deep concern and compassion for others, and he seems to be endowed with an unusual inner strength and will power.[4] However, there is no fixed or definitive way in which the form-body appears. Depending upon his own personal character and the dispositions and inclinations of those with whom he is involved, a Buddha may assume a variety of aspects: peaceful and beatific, stern and wrathful, joyous and youthful, maternal and loving, kinglike and powerful, and so forth. But regardless of the particular appearances assumed, the underlying intention and aim of the form-body is to communicate to others through whatever means are available the way to a more meaningful, authentic and joyous existence. Thus the 'form-body' does not describe merely the physical aspect of a Buddha, but it refers to his optimum mode of being-in-the-world-with-others.

The form-body is grounded in the ontological structure of being-with-others. It is the fullest expression of concern for others and is realized primarily through the practices of method. Through its actualization, the aspiration of an awakening mind to be of the utmost possible benefit to others is fulfilled. It is only when the optimum mode of being is realized that one achieves the capacity to spontaneously act in such a way that one's every word and deed serves to intimate to others the possibility of experiencing a much fuller and richer existence. In this way the form-body is said to be the actualization of meaningful being-for-others.

Moreover, the form-body is usually described as having two principal aspects; the so-called 'enjoyment-body' (sambhogakāya) and the 'emanation-body' (nirmānakāya). These designations refer to the two principal modes of being through which we relate ourselves to others, namely: speech and embodied action. Hence what is called the 'enjoyment-body' is actually the optimal mode of communicating our experiences to others through speech. Since speech is intimately connected to thought, we can further understand the enjoyment-body to represent not only the vocal expressions themselves but the entire structure and process of the coherent articulation of meaning. As such it mediates, so to speak, between the inarticulate domain of aloneness in which the dharma-body experience is rooted and the more audible and visible manifestations of being that are directly accessible to others. The emanation-body is the most concrete manifestation of the optimum mode of being. However, it should not be simplistically understood as representing the mere physical form, but rather the embodim ˙ ˙t of man in all its expressive power.

In this way we can see how the doctrine of the 'three-fold-Buddha-body' (*trikāya*) is not describing three separate entities but three stages in the optimal process of unfolding from aloneness into participation, from formlessness into form. The silent depths of personal experience (dharma-body) find progressive expression through ideas and words (enjoyment-body) and are finally embodied in actions (emanation-body). An awareness of this process, which, it should be remembered, is grounded in a corresponding pattern of our present existence, helps shed light on the traditional representations of the Buddha in Mahāyāna Buddhism. The dharma-body, being formless, is never concretely depicted in images. The enjoyment-body, occurring at the level of ideas and collective images, is depicted in ideal Buddha figures, which have, however, not yet assumed concrete individual forms. It is only the emanation-body that is fully individualized and is thus depicted in the aspect of ordinary men and women.

Buddhahood is described as the attainment of a state of non-abiding nirvāna.[5] This refers to the fact that the optimum mode of being abides neither in the frustrating cyclic condition of samsāra nor in the quietistic absorption of nirvāna. Samsāra and nirvāna are two antithetical conditions of existence both of which hinder the fullest possible actualization of human potential. But although Buddhahood cannot be reduced to either one of these conditions, it nevertheless has access to them both. The dharma–body experiences the spiritual freedom and peace of nirvāna, and simultaneously the form–body actively participates in the lives of those bound in samsāra. It must be stressed, however, that the optimum state of being is not comprised of two independent and separate aspects. It is the inseparable unity of optimum being–alone and optimum being–with. In Buddhahood too one cannot avoid the paradoxical condition of being inescapably alone and at the same time inescapably in a world with others.

17. Is the Buddha Still Alive?

The greatest danger inherent in any presentation of Buddhism is that of unconsciously creating an unbridgeable gulf between the concrete living Buddha and the abstract ideal Buddha. Nowadays, in many traditional schools of Buddhism, the man who walked throughout Northern India with a group of disciples, begged for food, gave clear and practical teachings, and finally died of dysentery, seems to have been forgotten. In his place one finds a semi–divine being who is visualized as bearing numerous extraordinary physical characteristics, and whose life is described in fantastic mythical imagery. The essentially human element of the Buddha is dissolved in an impressive, but humanly unobtainable, idealized state of being. Simultaneously with this gradual process of abstraction, the concrete human Buddha slowly fades away and dies.

Surely the purpose of all the various trends and movements in Buddhist thought is to clarify the nature of the Buddha, the significance of his experience, and the meaning of his life for others. However, these attempts at clarification are constantly subjected to a strong counter-tendency to project ideas away from man and set them up as self-existent values in their own right. Institutionalization, in which one tradition of interpretation alone is taken as final and authoritative, creates the fertile soil that encourages this tendency to idealization. The goal of the adherents of the Buddhist community becomes more and more that of defending and upholding a particular set of beliefs and creeds, and less and less that of experientially discovering the meaning and purpose of human life In such an atmosphere Buddha recedes further and further away from man and becomes a shining object of worship, standing for all that is good and noble, while man sinks deeper into the darkness of beginningless ignorance and evil, separated by countless lifetimes from the realization of his ideal. It is at this point that Feuerbach's criticism of religion is valid. In *The Essence of Christianity* he remarks that

"It is essential to observe, and this phenomenon is an extremely remarkable one, characterizing the very core of religion, that in proportion as God becomes more *ideally* human, the greater becomes the apparent difference between God and man. To enrich God, man must become poor; that God may be all, man must become nothing." [6]

Although the context of Feuerbach's critique is Christianity his insight into the psychology of the institutionalized religious attitude is equally applicable to Buddhism. In an over-institutionalized and uncreative context, whether Christian, Buddhist, or whatever, the mind tends to project the object of its concern further and further away from itself.

How then is this tendency towards projecting the

central concern of religious life, i.e., Buddha, into the realm of unobtainable ideals to be prevented? The root of this problem lies neither in the need of the human mind to construct systems of interpretation nor in the institutions that are subsequently founded upon them. It is essential to the growth and continuity of spiritual life that the meaning of the religion is constantly rearticulated in a language and way of thinking that are compatible with the social and cultural conditions of the times. Likewise the community of faith requires a common conceptual and symbolic field of reference in order to maintain harmony and mutual understanding within itself. Thus systems of interpretation as well as institutions are both necessary and unavoidable. The real root of this problem is found in our craving to find permanent security in something distinct from and unrelated to ourselves. Our initial turning to Buddhism may have been motivated by the discovery that no lasting security can be found however much we manipulate the external elements of the world. But the danger now is that instead of fleeing to a situation composed of material entities, we simply change direction and flee to an internal situation composed of immaterial entities. We become fascinated by the complex inner coherence of a belief structure, the perfection and supernatural qualities of a deified Buddha, and the promise of salvation in an afterlife. But all we are really doing is repeating the same inauthentic processes of flight from ourselves and absorption in a world of particular entities. We construct a castle within our minds out of the concepts and symbols of Buddhism and retreat into that. However, a castle will only afford us genuine security if its walls are solid and inpenetrable. Hence, we feel safe only when we are able to convince ourselves that the concepts and symbols of *our* belief structure are eternally valid and irrefutable. In this way, in order to maintain the sense of security we have achieved, we center our concern on establishing to ourselves and others the unique validity and superiority of our particular beliefs. It is easy to see how such an attitude would gradually cause people to elevate the contents of their belief to a successively higher, more idealized status as a means of confirming the unsurpassability and greatness of their tradition. The inevitable consequence of this process is that man comes to be regarded as more and more insignificant the more the perfection of the ideal is emphasized.

To prevent this tendency towards idealization from alienating man from the aim of his existential concern, it is important to never allow the elements of the belief structure to become fixed and opaque, thereby assuming an inherent value in themselves. The immediate danger of this tendency is that we proceed to naively translate the genuine existential problem that initially caused us to turn to Buddhism into a set of logical and technical problems that appear within the belief structure. In doing so we convince ourselves that we are authentically confronting the dilemmas of our existence, whereas in fact we are merely justifying to ourselves another inauthentic flight into a realm of particular entities. We deceive ourselves into assuming that through resolving the contradictions and ambiguities found in the teachings, we will automatically resolve the contradictions and ambiguities found in existence, and that though answering the questions implied within the body of dogma, we will discover an answer to the questions implied in life. This is an essentially futile exercise, the emptiness of which may be suddenly revealed in an unguarded moment when the ontological anxiety we thought we were dealing with reveals itself to us with even greater menace than before.

In order for the conceptual and symbolic structure

of Buddhism to enable man to actualize his own essential possibilities, instead of alienating him from them, it is necessary that the structure remains *transparent*. This means that we need to always look *through* it towards the possibilities of existence that it refers to and not *at* it. The concepts and symbols of which the structure is composed should be seen as clear lenses through which to bring ourselves, our questions, and our aims into focus. With the basis of such an attitude we are constantly grounded in the sensuous reality of our human existence, and the danger of indulging in flights of abstraction is thereby greatly diminished. In this way the belief structure becomes subordinate to the aims of man, instead of man becoming subordinate to the aim of justifying the structure. Consequently an appreciation of the relative nature of the structure emerges. It becomes clearer that its particular form is always determined by numerous cultural and historical factors that play no part at all in its essential role as a means of answering the questions implied within our very being-in-the-world. Hence it ceases to be something fixed, sacred, and unalterable. It is a means towards a greater end, and, as such, must serve that end by assuming the form that is the most compatible with and effective in the particular cultural environment where it finds itself.

The concepts, dogmas, and symbols of Buddhism have meaning only in relation to the life of man. All the practices of Buddhism are simply ways of actualizing the potentialities of human existence that dwell within us here and now. Buddha is nothing but the optimum mode of being possible for man in his present condition. It is only through remaining firmly within this human context that a meaningful unalienated perspective can be gained with regard to the Buddhist teachings. The true spirit of Buddhism is that of a humanized religion. Every central event in its history is characterized by a resurgence of this humanistic spirit as a countercurrent to the tendency towards idealization. Its very inception was marked by Shākyamuni's total rejection of the then current Brahmanical hypostatization of the essence of man (*ātman*) into an entity subsisting independently of the body and mind. His original teachings stressed that the aim of spiritual life is achieved through constant mindfulness of the psycho-physical constituents of man, and not through speculative inquiry concerned with either a divine absolute or a self, which are essentially alien from the concrete reality of human existence. The emergence of the Mahāyāna schools was likewise a reaction against the over-emphasis on the isolated quietude of nirvāna in which the Arhat remained inaccessible to and remote from others. By stressing the ideal of the Bodhisattva, the thrust of Buddhism was again placed in the concrete sphere of human existence. So much so that Chandrakīrti remarks that the Bodhisattva's joy upon hearing a cry for help exceeds even the nirvanic bliss of the Arhat.[7]

However, the Mahāyāna traditions also succumbed to the tendency towards idealization. Largely because of their preoccupation with speculative metaphysics, the Buddha and even the Bodhisattvas were imagined as radiant ethereal beings exerting their quasi-divine influence as invisible spectators of, rather than living participants in, the human drama. Once again the goal and meaning of spiritual life became more and more remote and unreachable. However, through the emergence of Tantrism in India and Tibet, and Ch'an (Zen) in China and Japan, Buddhism was reestablished in the dimensions of concrete human existence. A principal feature of the Tantric teachings is that Buddha is identified with one's own human spiritual teacher. And to further emphasize this point that Buddahood is a concrete mode of human being, and not

an inaccessible ideal, the realized Siddha is often portrayed as living the most humble and ordinary existence. For example, Saraha was an arrowmaker, Tilopa
a beggar, and Marpa a farmer.[8] Similar accounts
abound in the literature of Ch'an Buddhism. The enlightened Zen Master is typified as someone who frequently exaggerates the quirks, the ambiguities and
the contradictions found in everyday human life. To
conceive of Buddha as an idealized state of being
standing in any way outside the sphere of actual human existence is regarded as anathema. Such attitudes
are condemned in the most forceful language: "If you
see the Buddha on the road, kill him!"[9]

Nowadays, to a large extent, the very factors of
over-rigid institutionalization and idealization against
which the original Tantric and Zen Masters rebelled
have come to dominate the Tantric and Zen traditions
themselves. Apart from a few exceptional cases, the
spontaneity and depth of human feeling that was so
characteristic of the founders of these traditions has
been swallowed up in elaborate ritual and dry formalism. The possibility of living Buddhahood has been
gradually pushed further and further out of reach and
has been supplanted by uncritical acceptance of and
obedience to an objectified tradition. The early Sid-
dhas have been transformed into illusion–like manifestations of transhuman Buddha principles. Even the
living teachers in whom Buddha is asserted to be present have been elevated to such unreachable heights
that Buddhahood, despite the fact that it is claimed to
be embodied here and now, has again become an alien
ideal. The kōans, spontaneously uttered by the first
Zen Partriarchs in moments of direct human encounter, have been systematically recorded and are method-
ically passed on from generation to generation. And
both traditions have become so strongly identified
with their cultural forms that it has become exceed-

ingly difficult for most of their proponents to distinguish between what is essential to the religious experience and what is merely a cultural accretion.

One can detect a movement underlying the developments of Buddhism similar to the process of breathing. Inhalations are followed by exhalations. Yet between the two are moments of changeover when neither inhalations nor exhalations are taking place. Although usually unnoticed, these tiny moments are as equally indispensible to the process of breathing as the more obvious and lengthy in-breaths and out-breaths themselves. Especially crucial is the point after an exhalation and before the next inhalation. The continuation or the cessation of the life of the organism hangs in that moment. The inhalations can be compared to the inspired rise and growth of a particular Buddhist tradition, and the exhalations to its decline into fixed, lifeless forms. The tradition lives and flourishes only when it is firmly grounded in the context of human existence and thus has immediate existential significance for the community of faith. It reaches a peak though, pauses for a glorious moment, and starts to exhale, expelling the air that it had inhaled deep into itself away into the space of idealized abstraction, thereby alienating man from the realization of his inner potential. Both prior to the inhalation, containing the vital spark of its inspiration, and subsequent to the exhalation, containing the possibility of extinction, lies a crucial moment of sheer uncertainty. It is in such moments that the key events in the development of Buddhism occur. The principal event was the presence of Shākyamuni himself, who initially established the early schools such as the Theravāda. The subsequent key events were the advent of the Mahāyāna, and within that tradition, the phenomena of Tantrism and Ch'an. These four moments were life-giving sparks that followed periods of spiritual deadness and evoked new waves of authentic religious enthusiasm. But today the life-breath of these traditions has reached the final moments of an exhalation.

We are approaching, perhaps we have already entered, the crucial moment of uncertainty at which, if the organism of Buddhism is not restimulated by a fresh spark of life, it will gradually come to rest, its energies being incorporated into other fields. This is a critical period in which the traditional forms of Buddhism are being uprooted from their ancient habitats and confronted with the world-dominating movements of science, technology, and socialism. The world-views in which they have acquiesced for centuries are being challenged from all sides. But the survival of Buddhism in this world as an effective counterbalance, on no matter how small a scale, to the oppressive forces of materialism and dogmatic political ideologies is not dependent upon the perpetuation of any institutionalized tradition. It is not a question of reforming certain elements of the traditional belief structures, casting out what seems to be anachronistic and emphasizing whatever seems appealing to the modern spirit. This approach has simply a cosmetic effect, which is not only misleading but often has the negative consequence of reducing Buddhism to a mere system of psychology or ethics. No particular element of any internally consistent system can ever be fully significant when isolated from its relation to the whole from which it derives its meaning. Reforms and modifications of a religious structure are only effective when the underlying cultural, social, economic, and historical conditions in which that structure originated remain basically unchanged. The idea that one can effectively transplant even modified versions of Theravāda, Tibetan or Japanese Buddhism into the environment of the modern world is unrealistic.

However, the very fact that so many diverse yet

firmly established traditions were able to develop under quite different cultural conditions in the past indicates a strong trans-cultural flexibility in the essential nature of the Buddhist experience. It is true that the differences in outlook and culture between a modern industrial society and a traditional Buddhist society are far greater than those that ever existed between the countries between which the interchange of Buddhist ideas originally occurred. But it is also true that the fundamental questions posed to man by the sheer fact of his being in the world are no less of a mystery today than they were a thousand years ago. The basic problems of meaninglessness, anxiety, despair, suffering, and death are just as present and urgent now as they have ever been. The extent of the cultural and historical gap only indicates the extent to which a radical reformulation of the Buddhist answer to man's existence needs to take place if Buddhism is to play a meaningful role in the life of man today.

The survival of Buddhism depends upon the experiential rediscovery of its innermost spark, and the articulation of that experience in a language that speaks directly to the deepest hopes and fears of present-day man. Central to this task is the firm reestablishment of Buddha within the living sphere of concrete human existence. This entails placing constant emphasis on the essential humanity of Shākyamuni and the exclusively human structures of being to which his teachings, as well as those of his followers, refer. Buddhism should provide a model of the optimum possible mode of human life, and cease to focus on the eventual achievement of distant intangible ideals. In addition, these teachings need to be formulated as answers that correlate to the principal existential questions posed today. It is only through constantly keeping the questions alive that the answers are likewise kept alive and not formalized as values in themselves. Yet however critical one may be of certain institutionalized forms, this process of rearticulation needs to be solidly grounded in the living continuity of the Buddhist traditions. It is only in an atmosphere of heartfelt respect for those who are passing on the lifeblood of Buddhism that criticism and reinterpretation can have any genuine value. Unless they are an expression of faith trying to understand itself, they will be nothing more than empty academic chatter.

*

NOTES

CHAPTER ONE

1. Gabriel Marcel, *Homo Viator: Introduction to a Metaphysics of Hope*, p. 61. Quoted in John MacQuarrie, *Twentieth Century Religious Thought*, p.360.
2. For a further analysis of this distinction, see Erich Fromm, *To Have or To Be?*, also, Gabriel Marcel, *Having and Being*.
3. T.S. Eliot, *The Hollow Men*, from *Collected Poems 1909–1962*, p.89.
4. Cf. Matt. 21: 12-14.
5. Cf. Paul Tillich, *The Dymanics of Faith*.
6. This account is in accordance with Aśvaghosa's *Buddhacarita*. Certain elements of this story are the products of mythical imagination rather than historical fact. Neither was Siddhārtha a prince nor his father a king. It seems probable that the Shakyas were an independent tribe belonging to a larger confederation which was governed by a council of elders drawn from the different tribal groups. The Buddha's father was the titular head of such a council who merely assumed the title *rājā* (king) for the duration of his incumbency. Thus, although Siddhārtha probably lived a comfortable existence by the standards of his time, it should not be imagined that he was actually brought up in a palace.
7. *The Middle Length Sayings*, Tr. I.B. Horner, Vol. I, p. 207 (abridged).

CHAPTER TWO

1. Attributed to the Buddha, quoted in Tzong Khapa, *drang. nges. legs. bshad. snying. po.*, Collected Works, Vol. *pha.*, p. 482.

2. Cf. the discussion of the concept of correlation in Paul Tillich, *Systematic Theology*, Vol. I, p.59 seq.
3. This example is taken from William Barrett, *The Illusion of Technique*, p.134.
4. Cf. Paul Tillich, *The Courage to Be*, p. 63–68.
5. Ludwig Feuerbach, *The Essence of Christianity*, p.7.
6. See also section 16.
7. Cf. Arnold Toynbee, *Mankind and Mother Earth*, p. 251, 272, 286, 292–3, 318–9.
8. Cf. N. Dutt, *Buddhist Sects in India*, p.218 seq.
9. Cf. F.D. Lessing and A. Wayman, *Introduction to the Buddhist Tantric Systems*, p.22n.
10. See also section 17.
11. This is an idea from the Protestant Theologian Rudolf Bultman. Cf. John MacQuarrie, *An Existentialist Theology*, p.5.
12. Cf. John MacQuarrie, *Principles of Christian Theology*, p.1.

CHAPTER THREE

1. Paul Tillich, *Systematic Theology*, Vol. I, p.61.
2. For an introduction to modern phenomenology, see, for example, Edmund Husserl's article, *Phenomenology*, or William Barrett, *The Illusion of Technique*, p. 116 seq.
3. Cf. John MacQuarrie, *An Existentialist Theology*, p.30
4. Cf. Paul Tillich's discussion of the ontological polarities of individualization and participation, *Systematic Theology*, Vol. I, p.174 seq.
5. The psychological consequences, specifically in terms of schizophrenia, of the disruption between the poles of being-alone and being-with are elaborated in R.D. Laing, *The Divided Self*, part I.
6. Shāntideva, *A Guide to the Bodhisattva's Way of Life*, (*Bodhicaryāvatāra*), (hereafter referred to as *Guide*) VIII: 32.
7. "Facticity" is a rendering of the German "Faktizität" and is further clarified in Martin Heidegger, *Being and Time*, p.235 seq.
8. Nino Langiuilli, *The Existentialist Tradition*, p.11.
9. Cf. John MacQuarrie, *An Existentialist Theology*, p.183.
10. Cf. Tzong Khapa, *lam.rim.chen.mo.*, p.117 seq., and Heidegger, *Being and Time*, p. 279 seq. (esp. sections 51-2).
11 Heidegger, *Being and Time*, p.294.

12. Cf Heidegger, *Being and Time*, p.219-24 for further clarification of the concept of falling'. The term 'particular entity' here corresponds to Heiddeger's *das Seiende* as opposed to *das Sein.*

13. Cf. Heidegger, *op. cit.*, p.163–8.

14. Tib: *ma.rig.pa.*, Skt *avidhyā.*

15. Being–itself (Tib· *chos.nyid.*, Skt: *dharmatā*) is concealed by ignorance, and our attention is focused exclusively on particular entities (Tib: *chos.*, Skt: *dharma.*)

16. Cf. Heidegger, *Being and Time*, p.228-35, and his essay, *What is Metaphysics?*, included in *Basic Writings*, p. 102.

17. Heidegger, *Being and Time*, p.235.

18. Aśvaghosa *Buddhacarita*, V:1 (my italics). I have slightly modified Johnson's translation in accordance with the Tibetan text.

19. Heidegger, *What is Metaphysics?*, included in *Basic Writings*, p. 108. 'Man's being' is my rendering of the original term *Dasein.*

20. Cf. Geshe Rabten, *The Mind and its Functions.* p.6.

21. Here I am interpreting the Buddhist concept of faith (Skt: *sraddhā*, Tib: *dad.pa.*) as a synthesis of its three principal aspects of lucid appreciation (Tib: *dang.ba.* = *mos.pa.*), longing (Tib: *'dod.pa.*), and conviction (Tib: *yid.ches.*). Cf. Geshe Rabten, *The Mind and its Functions*, ch.8, sec.I. My interpretation is influenced by Tillich's definition and explication of faith as the 'state of being ultimately concerned'. Cf. the illuminating account of the subject in Paul Tillich, *The Dynamics of Faith.*

22. Cf. Tzong Khapa, *lam.rim.chen.mo.*, p. 157 seq. The idea of hope (Tib: *re.ltos.byed.pa'i.blo.*) as the nature of refuge is taken from the Tibetan oral tradition.

23. Cf. Maitreya, *Mahāyānottarantraśastra.* I:21.

CHAPTER FOUR

1. Martin Heidegger, *Being and Time*, p. 160. The term 'human being' in the cited passage is my rendering of the original term *Dasein.*

2. Cf. Heidegger, *Being and Time*, p. 157.

3. Cf. John MacQuarrie, *Principles of Christian Theology*, p. 123.

4. The interpretation of the Greek definition, *zoion logon echon*

follows Martin Heidegger, *Being and Time*, p.47., (see also
the translator's footnote). The Buddhist definition is, in Tibetan, *smra.bshad.don.go*. I have been unable to trace its
source although it is common in the oral tradition.
5. *Dhammapada*, v.166.
6. Shāntideva, *Guide*. VIII: 113.
7. For more on an awakening mind (Tib: *byand.chub.kyi.sems*.
Skt: *bodhicitta*) see sec. 12; on method (Tib: *thabs*., Skt:
upāya) sec. 15; and the form–body (Tib: *gzugs.sku*., Skt:
rūpakāya) sec. 16.
8. Cf. Shāntideva, *Guide*, VIII: 90–187, also see sec. 12 below.
9. Shāntideva, *op.cit.*, VIII: 114.
10. Shāntideva, *op.cit.*, VIII: 99.
11. Tib: *rang.gcez.'dzin*.
12. For further details see Geshe Rabten, *The Mind and its Functions*, p.88-107.
13. Martin Buber, *I and Thou*, p.69.
14. For a further discussion of equanimity cf. Geshe Rabten, *The
Life and Teachings of Geshe Rabten, p. 154-9*.
15. Shāntideva, *Guide*, VIII: 95-6.
16. Tib: *gzhan.gces.'dzin*.
17. Shāntideva, *Guide*, VIII:94.
18. Shāntideva, *op.cit.*, VIII: 116, also cf. VIII:109.
19. Shāntideva, *op.cit.*, VIII: 141.
20. For more on meaningful being for oneself (Tib: *rang.don.*)
and meaningful being for others (Tib: *gzhan.don.*) see 16.

CHAPTER FIVE

1. Atīsha, *byang.chub.lam.gyi.sgron.ma*. (*bodhipathapradīpa*),
v.46.
2. Tib: *sangs.rgyas.chos.dang.tshogs.kyi.mchog.rnams.la/*
byang.chub.bar.du.bdag.ni.skyabs.sn.mchi./
bdag.gi.spyin.sogs.bgyi.pa'i.bsod.nams.kyis./
'gro.la.phan.phyir.sangs.rgyas.sgrub.par.shog. Source un-
known, popularly attributed to Atīsha.
3. Tib: *mthar.thug.theg.pa.gcig*., Skt: *ekayāna*.
4. Sadddharmapundarikasūtra, v.44. Cited in sGam.po.pa., *The
Jewel Ornament of Liberation*, p.6.
5. This distinction is based upon sGam.po.pa's treatment of the
six transcending functions in his *Jewel Ornament of Liberation*, p.148

6. *Dhammapada*, v.1. I have modified the translation slightly.
7. Both perception (Tib: *rtog.mod.kyi.blo.*) and conception (Tib: *rtog.bcas.kyi.blo.*) are further explained in Geshe Rabten, *The Mind and its Functions*, p.11-25.
8. Tib: *don.spyi.*
9. This example is taken from H.H. the XIV Dalai Lama, Tenzin Gyatso, *The Buddhism of Tibet and the Key to the Middle Way*, p.62.
10. Tib: *mi.rtag.pa.rtag.par.'dzin.pa./ sdug.bsngal.ba.bde.bar. 'dzin. pa./ bdag.med.pa.dbag.tu.'dzin.pa.*
11. Jean-Paul Sartre, *Nausea*, p.182-8.
12. For 'mood' I have in mind the Heideggerian concept of *Befindlichkeit*. See *Being and Time*, p.172-9.
13. Tib: *bdag.'dzin.*
14. Tzong Khapa, *lam.rim.bsdus.don.*, included in *Collected Works*, vol. *kha, thor.bu.* section, p.134. For further reading on concentration and wisdom, see Geshe Rabten, *The Life and Teachings of Geshe Rabten*, p.165-97, and the Dalai Lama's *Key to the Middle Way*, (see note 9 above).
15. Cf. Shāntideva, *Guide*, chapter V throughout.
16. Cf. Shāntideva, op.cit., V:12-14, and chapter VI throughout.
17. Shāntideva, op. cit., VII: 63, 66,
18. Cf. Shāntideva, op. cit., chapter VII throughout. It could be argued that enthusiasm pertains as equally to the actualization of authentic being–alone as to that of authentic being-with. This possibility is confirmed in Maitreya's *Mahāyānasūtrālamkāra*, XVI: 7, cited in *The Jewel Ornament of Liberation*, p. 148

CHAPTER SIX

1. An account of Tê-shan given in D.T. Suzuki, *Essays in Zen Buddhism, 2nd Series*, p.51.
2. Cf. Maitreya, *Mahāyānottaratantrashastra*, I: 7.
3. *Pitāputrasamāgamasūtra*, cited in Tzong Kapa, *dbu.ma. dgongs.pa.rab.gsal.*, Collected Works, vol. *ma.* p.216.
4. Cf. Maitreya, *Mahāyānottaratantrashastra*, I: 7-8. These three qualities are personified in the Bodhisattva forms of Mañjushrī, Avalokiteśvara, and Vajrapāni respectively.
5. Tib: *mi.gnas.pa'i.mya.ngan.las.'das.pa.*
6. Ludwig Feuerbach: *The Essence of Christianity*, p.16.
7. Chandrakīrti, *Madhyamakāvatāra*, I:18

8. Cf. the biographical sections in H.V. Guenther, *The Life and Teachings of Nāropa*. Of especial note are the accounts of the meetings between Nāropa and Tilopa, and Marpa and Nāropa.

9. A well-known Zen aphorism.

✱

BIBLIOGRAPHY

(The reference for the entries marked 'P' are to the Peking edition of the Tibetan Tripitaka published by the Suzuki Research Foundation, Tokyo–Kyoto, 1956)

Aśvaghosa. *Buddhacarita.*

Atīsha. *byang.chub.lam.gyi.sgron.ma.* (*bodhipathapradīpa*) P.

Barrett, William. *The Illusion of Technique.* London: William Kimber & Co. 1979.

Buber, Martin. *I and Thou.* Tr. Walter Kaufmann. Edinburgh: T.T. Clark, 1979.

Buddha, *Saddharmapundarīkasūtra* (*dam.chos.pad.ma.dkar.poi. mdo.*) P.781, vol.30.

———. *Dhammapada.* Tr. Narada Maha Thera. Calcutta: Mahabodhi Society, 1970.

———. *Pitāputrasamāgamasūtra* (*yab.dang.sras.mjal.ba'i.mdo.*) P. 760., vol.23.

———. Majjhima–Nikāya. Ed. and Tr. Horner, I.B. *The Middle Length Sayings.* London: Luzac, 1954.

Chandrakīrti. *Madhyamakāvatāra* (*dbu.ma.la.'jug.pa*) P.5262, vol.98.

Dostoyevsky, F. *The Idiot.* Tr. David Magarshack. London: Penguin, 1955.

Dutt, N. *Buddhist Sects in India.* Delhi: Motilal Banarsidass, 1978.

Eliot, T.S. *Collected Poems 1909–1962.* London: Faber and Faber, 1974.

Feuerbach, Ludwig. *The Essence of Christianity.* Ed. and abridged by E. Graham Waring and F.W. Strothmann. New York: Ungar, 1957.

Fromm, Erich. *To Have or To Be?* New York: Harper and Row, 1976.

sGam.po.pa. *The Jewel Ornament of Liberation.* Tr. H.V. Guenther. London: Rider, 1970.

Guenther, H.V. *The Life and Teachings of Nāropa.* London: Oxford University Press, 1963.

Gyatso, Tenzin, H.H. the XIV Dalai Lama. *The Buddhism of Tibet and the Key to the Middle Way.* Tr. Jeffrey Hopkins. London: George Allen and Unwin, 1975.

Heidegger, Martin. *Basic Writings.* Ed. David Farrell Krell. London: RKP, 1978.

──────. *Being and Time.* Tr. John MacQuarrie and Edward Robinson, Oxford: Blackwell, 1962.

Husserl, Edmund. *Phenomenology.* From the 14th edition of the Encyclopedia Britannica, 1929.

Johnston, E.H. (ed. and tr.) *The Buddhacarita.* Delhi: Notilal Banarsidass, 1972.

Laing, R.D. *The Divided Self.* London: Pelican, 1965.

Langiuilli, Nino. (ed.) *The Existentialist Tradition.* New York: Anchor, 1971.

Lessing, F.D. and Wayman, A. *Introduction to the Buddhist Tantric Systems.* Delhi: Motilal Banarsidass, 1978.

MacQuarrie, John. *An Existentialist Theology.* London: Pelican, 1973.

──────. *Principles of Christian Theology.* London: SCM, 1966

──────. *Twentieth Century Religious Thought.* London: SCM, 1963.

Maitreya. *Mahāyānasūtrālamkāra* (*theg.pa.chen.po'i.mdo.sde. rgyan.*) P.5521, vol. 108.

──────. *Mahāyānottaratantraśastra.* (*theg.pa.chen.po'i.rgyud.bla. ma'i.bstan.bcos.*) P.5525, vol.108.

Marcel, Gabriel. *Having and Being.* Tr. Katherine Farrer. Westminster: Dacre, 1949.

──────. *Homo Viator: Introduction to a Metaphysics of Hope.* Chicago: Regency, 1952.

Rabten, Geshe. *The Life and Teachings of Geshe Rabten.* Tr. and ed. B. Alan Wallace. London: George Allen and Unwin, 1980.

──────. *The Mind and its Functions.* Tr. and ed. Stephen Batchelor. Switzerland: Tharpa Choeling, 1978.

Sartre, Jean-Paul. *Nausea.* Tr. Robert Baldick. London: Penguin, 1965.

Shāntideva. *A Guide to the Bodhisattva's Way of Life* (*Bodhicaryāvatāra*) Tr. Stephen Batchelor. Dharamsala: I ibrary of Tibetan Works and Archives, 1979.

────── *Guide.* see: *A Guide to the Bodhisattva's Way of Life*

Suzuki, D.T. *Essays in Zen Buddhism, 2nd Series.* London: Rider, 1970.

Tillich, Paul. *The Courage to Be.* London: Fontana, 1962.

———. *The Dynamics of Faith.* New York: Harper and Row, 1958.

———. *Systematic Theology* (Three Volumes in One). Chicago· The University of Chicago Press, 1967.

Toynbee, Arnold. *Mankind and Mother Earth.* London: OUP, 1976.

Tzong Khapa. *dbu.ma.dgongs.pa.rab.gsal.*, Collected Works, vol. *ma.* Delhi: 1979.

———. *drang.nges.legs.bshad.snying.po.*, Collected Works, vol. *pha.* Delhi: 1979.

———. *lam.rim.chen.mo.*, Collected Works, vol. *pa.* Delhi: 1979.

———. *lam.rim.bsdus.don.*, Collected Works, vol. *kha.* Delhi: 1979.

GLOSSARY

ARHAT (*Skt.*) A Buddhist saint who has gained final liberation through the attainment of Nirvāna and is thereby no longer bound to the frustration and suffering of Samsāra. Although this state of being is a characteristic of the Buddha, it has come to typify the Hīnayāna ideal of sainthood in contrast to the Mahāyāna ideal of the Bodhisattva.

ASHOKA (264–232 B.C.) An Indian King who politically united the Indian sub-continent and was renowned for his devotion to and propogation of Buddhism.

ATISHA (982–1054) An Indian scholar and saint who visited Tibet in the eleventh century and founded the Kadampa school, a reformed tradition that tried to steer a middle course between the diverse sects in Tibet at that time. He emphasized a graduated path to enlightenment that incorporated and systematized all the various teachings of Buddhism. He had a great influence on Tzong Khapa, and his school is often seen as a precursor to the later Gelukpa tradition.

BODHISATTA (*Pali*) See: BODHISATTVA

BODHISATTVA (*Skt.*) The Mahāyāna ideal of sainthood. Someone who has developed an awakening mind (*bodhicitta*) and devotes his life to the task of achieving Buddhahood for the sake of others.

CH'AN (*Chinese*) See: ZEN.

CHANDRAKIRTI (c. A.D. 600) An Indian Buddhist scholar who clarified and developed the Mādhyamaka philosophy of Nāgārjuna.

DEVADATTA The cousin of Shākyamuni who denounced the Buddha and tried to usurp control of the Buddhist Sangha.

DHARMA (*Skt.*) (1) The practice of religion in general; in this context the practice of Buddhism. (2) The teachings of Buddhism. (3) When written *dharma*, any existent phenomenon.

DHARMAKĀYA *(Skt.)* Literally: 'the Dharma-Body' The Buddha-mind, the state of optimum being-for-oneself. See sec. 16.

GELUKPA *(Tib.)* The tradition of Tibetan Buddhism founded by Tzong Khapa which became the largest and most powerful school in Tibet. It is characterized by placing emphasis on gaining a sound theoretical understanding of Buddhism before proceeding to advanced forms of meditation.

GUPTA *(Skt.)* The name of a powerful Indian empire lasting from A.D. 320 until A.D. 490.

HĪNAYĀNA *(Skt.)* Literally: 'the lesser vehicle'. A pejorative title given by the Mahayanists to the earlier schools of Buddhism such as the Theravāda. These schools were considered 'lesser' or 'inferior' because of their emphasis on the isolated detachment of the Arhat, in contrast to the active participation in the world of the Bodhisattva.

JĀTAKA *(Skt.)* A section of the Buddhist Canon which recounts the stories of the Buddha in his previous incarnations.

KŌAN *(Jap.)* Chinese: KUNG-AN. Literally 'a public case'. Usually it involves an anecdote of the encounter between a Zen Master and a disciple in which an answer, often highly paradoxical, is given to a certain question and occasions the enlightenment of the disciple. The main point of the Kōan is subsequently used as an object of meditation in Zen Buddhism.

KUSHANA *(Skt.)* The name of an Indian empire lasting from A.D. 48 until approximately A.D. 220.

MAHĀSAMGIKA *(Skt.)* One of the eighteen early sub-schools of Buddhism, usually considered in the Hīnayāna category.

MAHĀYĀNA *(Skt.)* Literally: 'the great vehicle'. A name for the later schools of Buddhism that emphasized the ideal of the Bodhisattva. It started emerging in a systematized form during the first and second centuries A.D. It is the form of Buddhism that prevailed in Tibet, Mongolia and China. It is still alive in Japan, Korea and Nepal.

MARPA (1012-1099) The founder of the Kagyupa school of Tibetan Buddhism that, in contrast to the Gelukpa, lays less stress on philosophical study and encourages an early entry into Tantric meditation. He was a disciple of Nāropa (1016-1100) and the teacher of Milarepa (1052-1135).

MAURYA *(Skt.)* The name of the Indian empire created by Ashoka that lasted from 322 B.C. until 232 B.C.

NĀGĀRJUNA (c. A.D. 150) An Indian Buddhist scholar and saint who founded the Mādhyamaka philosophy of Shūnyatā and helped initiate the emergence of the Mahāyāna.

NIBBĀNA *(Pali)* See: NIRVĀNA.

NIRVĀNA *(Skt.)* The unconditioned state of cessation in which all the operations of Samsāra are absent. It is the goal of the Arhat in which complete freedom from all samsāric involvements is achieved.

PALI CANON The earliest compilation of the Buddha's discourses.

RŪPAKĀYA *(Skt.)* Literally 'the Form-Body'. The way in which the Buddha is present to others, the state of optimum being-for-others. See sec. 16.

SAMSĀRA *(Skt.)* The inauthentic mode of existence in which one's actions are motivated by disturbing conceptions *(klesha)* rooted in ignorance *(avidhyā)*. It is characterized by anxiety, frustration, and suffering.

SANGHA *(Skt.)* The Buddhist community of faith. In particular, those persons who have made significant progress along the path to enlightenment and are able to guide others.

SARAHA (c. A.D. 100) A well-known Indian Buddhist Tantric Master. Reputedly the teacher of Nāgārjuna.

SARVĀSTIVĀDA *(Skt.)* One of the eighteen early sub-schools of Buddhism, usually considered in the Hīnayāna category.

SHĀKYAMUNI (c.500 B.C.) Literally: 'The Mighty One of the Shākya Clan'. The historical Buddha Gautama.

SHĀNTIDEVA (c. A.D. 700) An Indian Buddhist scholar and saint renowned for his composition of *A Guide to the Bodhisattva's Way of Life (Bodhicaryāvatāra)*, a work that emphasizes the development of an awakening mind.

SHRĀVAKA *(Skt.)* Literally 'a hearer'. A name given to certain followers of the Hīnayāna tradition who seek their own liberation through the attainment of Nirvāna.

SHŪNYATĀ *(Skt.)* Literally 'voidness'. The absence of inherent self-existence; the ultimate mode of being of all phenomena through the understanding of which freedom from Samsāra can be achieved.

SIDDHA *(Skt.)* One who has gained enlightenment through Tantric practices.

SIDDHĀRTHA The name of Shākyamuni as a Prince before he attained Buddhahood.

TANTRA *(Skt.)* A discipline found in both Hindu and Buddhist traditions that makes use of certain physical energies as an aid to progress along the spiritual path. It is a practice associated with visualization techniques, mantra recitation, breathing, and other yogic exercises. Buddhist Tantra dates from the early centuries A.D..

TATHĀGATA (*Skt.*) Literally 'One Who has Gone to Suchness'. An epithet for a Buddha.

THERAVĀDA (*Skt.*) One of the eighteen early sub-schools of Buddhism usually considered in the Hīnayāna category. Currently the major Buddhist tradition in Burma, Thailand, and Sri Lanka.

TILOPA (988-1069) A renowned Indian Tantric Master; the teacher of Nāropa. See: MARPA.

TZONG KHAPA (1357-1419) The founder of the Gelukpa school of Tibetan Buddhism. He further systemized the teachings of Atīsha and attempted to unify the Sūtra (i.e., exoteric) and Tantra teachings of Buddhism. One of his most influential works was the *Great Exposition on the Stages of the Path to Enlightenment* (*lam.rim.chen.mo.*)

ZEN (*Jap.*) Chinese: CH'AN. A school of Buddhism introduced into China by Bodhidharma (c. A.D. 500) and developed by such Masters as Hui Neng (A.D.637-713) which emphasizes the sudden realization of enlightenment through meditation. It is currently practiced in Japan and Korea.